INTRODUCTION TO TANTRA

INTRODUCTION ❀ TO TANTRA ❀
A Vision of Totality
LAMA YESHE

Compiled and Edited by Jonathan Landaw

Wisdom Publications • Boston

WISDOM PUBLICATIONS
199 Elm Street,
Somerville, Massachusetts 02144-3195 USA

Library of Congress Cataloging-in-Publication Data

Thubten Yeshe, 1935–84
    Introduction to tantra : a vision of totality / Lama
Thubten Yeshe ; compiled and edited by Jonathan Landaw.
        p.   cm.
    Includes bibliographic references.
    ISBN 0–86171–021–5 (pbk.) :
      1. Religious life—Tantric Buddhism.   2. Tantric Buddhism—
China—Tibet.   3. Tibetan Tantric Buddhist life.   I. Landaw,
Jonathan.   II. Title.
BQ8936B.T48   1987
294.3'444—dc20   89–163841

0 86171 021 5

02 01 00 99 98
11 10 9   8   7

Contents

Preface

The material that makes up this introduction to the often misunderstood world of buddhist tantra was compiled from teachings given between 1975 and 1983 by the late Tibetan monk Thubten Yeshe, known affectionately to his many students around the world as Lama Yeshe.

His biography has already appeared in the introduction to *Wisdom Energy*, a series of lectures selected from the 1974 tour of North America made by Lama Yeshe and his chief Tibetan disciple and heart-son, Lama Thubten Zopa Rinpoche. To recount a few of its major points briefly here, Lama Yeshe was born near Lhasa at Tölung in 1935 and from the age of six attended Sera Je Monastery, where he received an extensive spiritual and academic education. After the Chinese take-over of Tibet in 1959, he completed his education at the Buxaduar refugee camp in north-east India and eventually settled near the Boudhanath stupa outside Kathmandu, Nepal.

It was in Nepal that his contact with Westerners began in earnest, and by 1971 Lama Yeshe and Zopa Rinpoche had founded the Nepalese Mahayana Centre Gompa on Kopan hill, the site of yearly meditation courses that have attracted an ever-growing number of students. These students were eventually to establish over thirty centres where Buddhism could be studied and practised in the West, and Lama Yeshe spent the last ten years of his life travelling to these and other centres providing teachings, organizational leadership and, perhaps most importantly, the inspiration of his own tireless example of benefiting others. Finally, on March 3,

1984 in the Cedars-Sinai Hospital in Los Angeles — at dawn on the morning of the Tibetan New Year — he succumbed to a serious heart ailment that had been threatening his life for more than twelve years.

The idea for this book arose as early as 1981, when Lama Yeshe said he felt there was a need for a work that would introduce buddhist tantra to the West in a non-technical, easy-to-understand way. Even though tantra is considered by the various Tibetan traditions to be the most profound and advanced of all buddhist teachings, he felt its central message to be simple and clear, and extremely relevant to twentieth century life. As he said on many occasions, the West has discovered how to tap so many powerful sources of energy in nature but still remains largely unaware of the tremendous force, even more powerful than nuclear energy, contained within each one of us. As long as this powerful internal energy lies undiscovered, our life is doomed to remain fragmented and purposeless, and we will continue to fall victim to the mental and emotional pressures so characteristic of our age. The practice of tantra, which is designed to take advantage of this hidden inner resource and utilize it to the maximum extent, offers us the best opportunity to overcome these pressures and transform our lives into the meaningful, integrated whole that we all desire.

According to Lama Yeshe, the practice of tantra is so suitable for the modern Western world because it is 'scientific.' In other words, tantra, far from being a system of dogma to be accepted on faith or authority, is in fact a practical, step-by-step exploration of the human condition leading to self-discovery, and its results are verifiable through our own observations and experience. It is this emphasis on direct experience that should make tantra appealing to the great number of Westerners who have long been disillusioned with paths demanding belief and blind faith. Furthermore, as the following chapters should make abundantly clear, tantra is a path of joy and affirmation, qualities so sadly lacking in many of the currently depleted forms of what were once powerful spiritual traditions.

In the winter of 1982–83, an editing retreat was held near Cecina, Italy, with the aim of going through the many transcripts of Lama Yeshe's tantric teachings in preparation for their eventual publication. The members of this retreat had available to them hundreds of lectures on tantra delivered by Lama Yeshe in English over the previous decade, and each member focused his or her attention on a teaching or group of teachings related to a particular tantric practice. As a result of their work and the work of later editors, a number of these transcripts have now been published in form and language only minimally altered from that originally employed by Lama Yeshe himself.

As well as working on a particular series of lectures, the editors also tried to identify the major introductory themes common to all of Lama Yeshe's teachings on tantra. Each transcript was examined with the view of discovering how these themes were dealt with in the individual teachings. In this way a large body of material was selected from many different sources and loosely arranged according to subject matter. At this point the editors concentrated on the material that dealt with the subject of tantra in general, leaving the more detailed explanations of specific practices for separate publication.

The compiler of this present work then edited and rearranged this selected material in an attempt to produce a coherent presentation. The resulting draft was then read to Lama Yeshe in Dharamsala, India, during April 1983 at which time he offered many corrections, additional explanations and suggestions for the improvement of both tone and subject matter. During that year he also continued to lecture around the world and selections from these lectures — most particulary those given in Pomaia, Italy and Boulder Creek, California — were edited into the manuscript.

It was my hope that the entire revised manuscript would be checked once again with Lama Yeshe, but this was not to be. For many months after his death my work on the manuscript came to an almost complete halt as I found it extremely difficult to face the task of editing his words while coming to terms with the sad but unalterable fact that I would not be hearing the sweet, laughter-filled voice that uttered these words ever again. Eventually, however, with the kind and extremely patient support of many friends, it was possible to bring the manuscript to its present state of completion and offer it here.

I cannot make this offering, however, without a few words of apology, or at least of explanation. No one who ever had the experience of listening to Lama Yeshe speak would think it possible to capture in print the extraordinary effect he had on people. Like so many great teachers, what he revealed through his presence itself was the spark that gave his teachings their immense power and effectiveness, much more so than the highly unorthodox and often un-grammatical language that he used. This present selection from his oral teachings — recast in more or less standard English — will therefore most likely strike those readers familiar with Lama Yeshe as a pale imitation of the original. Furthermore, there is no way in which a work such as this can claim to represent Lama Yeshe's definitive views on tantra. As the historical accounts testify concerning Shak-yamuni Buddha's original discourses themselves, Lama Yeshe's teachings could be understood on as many different levels as there were listeners. It would therefore be pre-sumptuous to think that any one interpretation of what he taught is the only interpretation possible. All a compiler or editor such as myself can do is listen intently to the lectures or tapes and read the transcripts carefully, and then present as clearly as possible what he hears inwardly while familiar-izing himself with the teachings. It is important to keep in mind, therefore, that if someone else had been working from the same tapes and transcripts, a book of very different tone and content would have resulted.

Lama Zopa Rinpoche was referring to this multifaceted quality of Lama Yeshe's teachings when he said, 'Most teachers like myself teach only what they themselves know and not so much according to the needs of the people. But for Lama, whenever he gave teachings nothing was fixed; he didn't just talk about one subject. In the audience there would be people with various problems – spiritual problems, personal problems, family problems – and Lama would speak to all of them. And so, after a one-hour talk from Lama everybody would have received some answer to their problems. In the beginning some might have come just to see how a Tibetan lama looks and others might have come sincerely wanting peace. When Lama had finished, they would all go home with a happy mind, with some solution to their problems.'

To put this in a way that relates directly to the subject matter of this present work, Lama Yeshe had the marvellous ability to touch in the people he contacted a centre of peace, wisdom and joy that they may have only dimly been aware of previously. Perhaps his most profound teaching was just this: that we each possess within ourselves not only the answer to our own problems but the potential to live our lives on a much higher level than we currently imagine possible. It was not just that Lama Yeshe gave every appearance of having fulfilled that potential within himself, although his example of continuous selfless giving, in spite of a defective heart that should have killed him many years ago, was surely a profound inspiration to all who knew him. Even more strikingly, he was able to inspire in his listeners a confidence that they, too, possessed similar unlimited potential waiting to be tapped.

Throughout this presentation of Lama Yeshe's introduction to the vast and profound subject of tantra, efforts have been made to keep technical terminology and historical references to a minimum. This has been done in accordance with Lama Yeshe's wishes in an attempt to convey the flavour of these teachings in as straightforward a manner as possible.

However, when technical terms have been used — whether English, Sanskrit or Tibetan – they have been noted in the glossary. And for those interested in exploring further the various topics raised in this work, a list of suggested readings, briefly annotated, will be found at the end.

The completion of this work would have been impossible without the contribution of a great many people, only a few of whom can be acknowledged here. My deepest thanks go first to the other members of the editing retreat at which the material for this book was first selected: Hermes Brandt, Lee Bray, Robyn Brentano, Stephen Carlier, Sharon Gross and Nick Ribush. During later stages of editing this material, the Aryatara family at Jaegerndorf and Munich gave unreservedly of their time and hospitality, as did the Philipsen family of Dronten, the Netherlands, and Geoff Jukes of London; the gratitude I feel for this kind and loving support cannot be easily expressed. Special thanks are also due to Yeshe Khadro whose encouragement and assistance proved invaluable. And finally to all those associated with Wisdom Publications — especially Robina Courtin, whose contributions benefited this work at every stage of its development — I would like to convey my deep appreciation for their patience during the many months it took for the manuscript of this book to be completed, as well as for their expert presentation of the final work.

JONATHAN LANDAW
Dronten
March, 1987

1 Basic Purity

The teachings and practices known as *buddhist tantra* can be traced back 2500 years to the time of Shakyamuni Buddha. The historical Buddha — to differentiate Shakyamuni from the many other awakened beings who have come before and after him — was born the Indian prince Siddhartha in the sixth century BC. According to traditional sources, he spent the first twenty-nine years of his life virtually imprisoned in the pleasure palaces built for him by his over-protective father, King Shuddhodana. Eventually, after becoming aware for the first time of sickness, old age and death, he escaped from his father's realm and began his search for the way to end all suffering and dissatisfaction.

For six years he engaged in strict asceticism and self-denial in an attempt to win control over his body and mind, only to discover that this extreme approach was as mis-guided as his previous life of sensual indulgence. Eventually, by following the middle path between indulgence and denial and avoiding all other extremes as well, he was able to uproot even the subtlest causes of suffering and ignorance from his mind, and thereby become a fully enlightened awakened one: a buddha. For the remaining forty-five years of his life, he taught this middle way approach to life and spiritual development in many different forms, each designed to suit the temperament and aptitude of a particular type of person.

Buddha's teachings — known in Sanskrit as *dharma*: that

which holds us back from suffering and its causes — contain thousands of different methods for overcoming the mental and physical obstacles to our happiness and well-being, and all fit within the two categories of *sutra* and *tantra*. There are differences between these two so-called vehicles (*yana*), but the foundation common to both *sutrayana* and *tantrayana* is the fundamentally pure nature of the mind.

FUNDAMENTAL PURITY OF THE MIND

According to the buddhist teachings, no matter how confused or deluded we may be at the moment, the underlying and essential nature of our being is clear and pure. In the same way that clouds can temporarily obscure but cannot damage the light-giving power of the sun, so too the temporary afflictions of body and mind — our confusion, anxiety and the suffering they cause — can temporarily obscure but cannot destroy or even touch the fundamentally clear nature of our consciousness. Dwelling deep within our heart, and within the hearts of all beings without exception, is an inexhaustible source of love and wisdom. And the ultimate purpose of all spiritual practices, whether they are called buddhist or not, is to uncover and make contact with this essentially pure nature.

When we have developed our own inner purity, inner compassion and inner love, we can then see the reflection of this purity and loving-kindness in others. But if we have not contacted these qualities within ourselves, we will see everyone as ugly and limited. For whatever we see every day in outer reality is actually nothing more than a projection of our own inner reality.

The existence of this deep, essentially pure nature of mind is not a matter of belief or of blind acceptance of dogma. It is a matter of experience. Countless people throughout history have discovered this great treasure of peace, love and wisdom within themselves. And countless great teachers and

guides have skilfully shown others how they too can discover their own deepest nature, and experience the unsurpassed happiness this discovery automatically brings.
Among these exceptionally kind spiritual guides is Shakyamuni Buddha, and the aim of all his many teachings and
methods is the fulfilment of our highest human potential.

According to buddhist terminology, the ultimate goal of
our individual human evolution is enlightenment or buddhahood. This state, which can be achieved by everyone, is
attained when all the delusions — greed, hatred, ignorance
and the like — presently obscuring our mind have been
completely removed and when all our positive qualities
have been fully developed. This state of complete fulfilment,
of full awakening, is characterized by unlimited wisdom,
unlimited compassion and unlimited skill, or power.

THE TANTRIC APPROACH

According to sutrayana, the path to fulfilment is a gradual
process of cleansing our mind of all its faults and limitations
and developing in their place such beneficial qualities as
love and wisdom. This path consists of creating specific
causes — behaving ethically, developing our powers of
concentration, training in meditative insight, and so forth —
for the future attainment of full awakening. Because of this
emphasis on creating causes for a future result, the gradual
approach of sutra is sometimes known as the *causal* vehicle
to enlightenment.

Compared to this gradual sutra approach, tantrayana is a
far speedier path to enlightenment. Although tantric practitioners do not neglect creating the same causes as the
followers of sutra, they take the future result of full spiritual
evolution as the very starting point in their path. To put this
in other words, the tantric *yogi* or *yogini* — as these supremely skilful practitioners are called in Sanskrit — learns to
think, speak and act *now* as if he or she were already a fully

enlightened buddha. Because this powerful approach brings the future result of full awakening into the present moment of spiritual practice, tantra is sometimes called the *resultant* vehicle to enlightenment.

According to tantra, perfection is not something that is waiting for us somewhere in the future. 'If I practise hard now maybe I will become a perfect buddha' or 'If I behave well in this life and act like a religious person, maybe some day I will go to heaven.' According to tantra, heaven is *now*! We should be gods and goddesses right now. But at present we are burdened with limiting concepts: 'Men are like this; women are like this; I am a certain way and there is nothing I can do about it' and so forth. This is why we have conflict within ourselves and with one another. All this conflict will dissolve as we train in the tantric point of view and recognize that each man is a complete man and each woman a complete woman. Furthermore, every man and woman contains both male and female energy. In fact, each one of us is a union of *all* universal energy. Everything that we need in order to be complete is within us right at this very moment. It is simply a matter of being able to recognize it. This is the tantric approach.

THE PRINCIPLE OF TRANSFORMATION

Speaking generally we can say that all the many practices of tantra involve the principle of transformation. As modern science has demonstrated, the physical universe with its infinite variety of phenomena − from the smallest sub-atomic particle to the largest galaxy − is in an unceasing state of transformation and evolution from one form of energy to another. Our own body and mind are also energy, and whether we are healthy or ill, mentally balanced or berserk, depends on whether our mental and physical energies are harmonious or not. Through the proper practice of tantra *all* of our energies, including the subtle yet very powerful energies we are not ordinarily aware of, are harnessed to accomplish the greatest of all transformations. This is our evolution from an ordinary, limited and deluded person trapped within the shell of a petty ego into a fully evolved, totally conscious being of unlimited compassion and insight.

How can we achieve such an extraordinary transformation? Where will we find the necessary resources to bring about such a profound change? We do not have far to look. We do not have to extract this force from the nucleus of an atom nor do we have to take a rocket ship into outer space and find it in some distant star. Instead, the basic energy involved in this profound process of tantric transformation is the energy of our own desires.

Shakyamuni Buddha

2 Desire and Happiness

DESIRE, FRUSTRATION AND SELF-CONTROL

We are living in a realm of desire. From the moment we wake up until the moment we fall asleep at night, and even throughout our dreams, we are driven by desire. Each of our senses is hungry for its own particular food. Our eye craves to see interesting shapes and colours; our ear wants to hear pleasing sounds; our nose actively sniffs out agreeable odours and turns away in disgust from smells that offend it; our tongue seeks exciting new tastes and our sense of touch is forever craving contact of one kind or another. This desire for sensory stimulation is so deeply ingrained that if we are isolated from sights, sounds, smells and so forth for long enough we begin to hallucinate them.

Our desires are not limited to the things we can see, hear, smell, taste and touch. Our mind itself runs after ideas as greedily as our tongue hungers for tastes. Abstractions such as knowledge, reputation, security and contentment are pursued with as much vigour as if they were things that could be held in the hand or seen by the eye. Desire is so pervasive, in fact, that it is doubtful whether there is anything that we do that is not motivated by it. No matter what field we may be involved in — whether it be business, sport or even spiritual pursuits — it is desire of one form or another that drives us to achieve success in it. Desires are such an integral part of our life that most people would consider life without them to be a living death.

Behind all of our desires is the wish to be happy. In this respect, everyone is exactly equal for we all want happiness − even though we may define it differently − and none of us wishes even the slightest suffering or disappointment. If we check up carefully we can see that all our actions are motivated by either the desire to experience what is pleasurable or the desire to avoid experiencing the unpleasant.

Yet in spite of all our wishes to have nothing but happiness our life is full of pain and dissatisfaction. Our prize possession that we worked so hard for either breaks, is lost or stolen, or simply ceases to give us pleasure. Our loving husband or wife soon becomes our worst enemy, or dies and leaves us forlorn. The job we coveted turns into a heavy burden that consumes all our time and energy. Our reputation is smeared, our smooth skin becomes wrinkled, our intelligence starts to fade. In all these ways, then, desired happiness eludes our grasp. Sometimes it seems that the more we try to be happy, the more miserable we become. From this point of view life seems to be a meaningless rat race; our efforts to find happiness lead us around in circles until we end up frustrated and exhausted.

Many different philosophers and spiritual teachers have described this circle of perpetual frustration and have offered advice on how to break free from it, or at least on how to put up with it. Shakyamuni Buddha, for example, referred to this condition of repeated dissatisfaction as *samsara* − a Sanskrit term meaning 'to circle,' − and prescribed many different methods for liberating ourselves from it. In the most well known of his teachings the source of all our problems and disappointments is said to be ignorantly produced desire itself. Liberation, or *nirvana*, is achieved by completely uprooting all such craving desire from our heart.

Because our eyes, ears, nose and so forth are the very gateways of desire, those wishing to break free and achieve liberation from this circle of suffering are encouraged to become especially distrustful of the five physical senses. These are to be recognized as exerting an unhealthy control over the mind and must be treated with the utmost caution.

The behaviour of someone following this path to individual liberation is therefore characterized by extreme self-control. The practitioner posts a strict guard at the door of the senses and is extremely suspicious of whatever wants to enter. If, for example, a desirous sight should appear — such as an attractive man or woman — the practitioner is advised to be alert to the possible danger of falling under its spell. When following this type of training we combat the tendency of running blindly after objects of attachment, and thereby falling victim to pain and disappointment, by teaching ourselves to focus on those aspects of the object that will reduce our desire for it. For instance, we can neutralize our longing for a beautiful person by concentrating on the unclean parts of his or her body. The aim of this type of practice is to keep desire from upsetting our minds and the intended result is to attain a peacefulness and tranquility that cannot be disturbed by the changing fortunes of our life.

Compared to a system like tantra, which actually uses the energy of desire, this cautious approach to the spiritual path is considered inferior. But this is not to say that such an approach has no value. On the contrary, it is crucial to know when it is appropriate to withdraw our attention from things that disturb our mind. However, if the only way we know how to deal with desirous objects is to avoid them, there will be a severe limit as to how far our spiritual practice can take us.

Tantra's approach is very different. Instead of viewing pleasure and desire as something to be avoided at all costs, tantra recognizes the powerful energy aroused by our desires to be an indispensable resource for the spiritual path. Because the goal is nothing less than the realization of our highest human potential, tantra seeks to transform *every* experience — no matter how 'unreligious' it may appear — into the path of fulfilment. It is precisely because our present life is so inseparably linked with desire that we must make use of desire's tremendous energy if we wish to transform our life into something transcendental.

Thus the logic of tantra is really very simple: our experience of ordinary pleasure can be used as the resource for attaining the supremely pleasurable experience of totality, or enlightenment. It is natural that qualities of the mind, when cultivated, produce something similar, not opposite, to themselves. This is true for both positive and negative states of mind. In the same way that dissatisfaction itself can never become satisfaction, misery does not naturally evolve into happiness. According to tantra, we cannot hope to attain our goal of universal and complete happiness by systematically making ourselves more and more miserable. This is contrary to the way things actually work. It is only by cultivating small experiences of calm and satisfaction now that we will be able to achieve our ultimate goal of peace and tranquility in the future. And similarly, it is only through the skilful use of desirous energy and by building up the habit of experiencing what we might call *true* pleasure that we can hope to achieve the everlasting bliss and joy of full illumination.

RELIGION AND THE REJECTION OF PLEASURE

It often seems, however, that there is a great contradiction between experiencing pleasure and following a spiritual, or religious, path. For many people, in fact, religion means nothing more than a denial or a rejection of the pleasurable parts of life. It is seen as saying 'no' to desire, 'no' to spontaneity, 'no' to freedom of expression. No wonder, then, that organized religion has such a bad name. Instead of being a method for transcending our limitations, religion itself is viewed as one of the heaviest forms of suppression. It is just another form of superstition to be overcome if we really want to be free. Unfortunately, the way in which many societies have used religion as a means of political oppression and control justifies this harsh judgement.

This view of religion as something that oppresses or

restricts our basic human nature is held not only by its critics but by many religious practitioners as well. There are a lot of people who feel that the proper way of following a spiritual discipline is by denying their simple humanity. They have become so suspicious of pleasure that they think there is actual value in being miserable: 'I am a religious person so I shouldn't enjoy myself.' Although their aim is to achieve some form of eternal peace and happiness they make a point of denying themselves the everyday pleasures of life. They view these pleasures as obstacles, hindrances to spiritual development, and if they happen to experience a small amount of pleasure, they feel uncomfortable. They cannot even eat a piece of chocolate without thinking they are sinful and greedy! Instead of accepting and enjoying such an experience for what it is, they tie themselves up in a knot of guilt and self-reproach: 'While so many people in the world are starving and miserable, how dare I indulge myself in this way!'

But all such attitudes are completely mistaken. There is no reason at all to feel guilty about pleasure; this is just as mistaken as grasping onto passing pleasures and expecting them to give us ultimate satisfaction. In fact, it is just another form of grasping, another way of locking ourselves into a limited view of who we are and what we can become. Such guilt is a perversion of spirituality, not a true spiritual attitude at all. If we were truly content with our situation — happy and peaceful when encountering good and bad conditions alike — there might be some real value in practising self-denial. It could be used beneficially to strengthen our sense of detachment or to help us understand what is truly important in our life. But we rarely deprive ourselves of something for the right reasons. We squeeze ourselves into a state of misery because we think that being miserable is itself somehow worthwhile. But it is *not* worthwhile. If we wallow in misery the only result is that we experience even more misery. On the other hand, if we know how to experience happiness without the polluted attitudes of either grasping attachment or guilt, we can cultivate deeper and deeper levels of this experience and eventually attain the inconceivable happiness of our full human potential.

If the fearful, self-restrictive approach that I have criticized is mistaken, then what is the skilful approach of someone seriously interested in realizing his or her highest potential? Stated simply, it is to keep the mind continuously in as happy and peaceful a condition as possible. Rather than letting ourselves follow habitual patterns of grasping, dissatisfaction, confusion, misery and guilt, we should try to improve our mind by developing deeper and deeper levels of understanding, more skilful control of our mental and physical energies, ever higher forms of happiness and bliss, and a better life. Such an approach makes much more sense than trying to reject our everyday experiences. *This* is the logic of tantra.

BUDDHA AND THE PATH OF ENJOYMENT

Certain episodes in the life of Shayamuni Buddha himself clearly demonstrate the superiority of an approach that uses desire-producing objects over a self-denying approach that forbids them. When he left the isolated and indulgent life of a prince at the age of twenty-nine and was just beginning his quest for the cessation of suffering, Buddha — then simply the bodhisattva Siddhartha — took up the discipline of extreme self-mortification. As some people still do in India today, he sought to uproot the causes of misery and dissatisfaction by beating his bodily senses into submission. He denied himself food and other comforts to such an extent that eventually he was little more than a skeleton. After six years of such self-deprivation he realized that this approach was fruitless. Instead of bringing him closer to his goal of transcendence, it was only making him too weak to think and meditate clearly.

At this point he decided to give up this inflexible approach and follow a path more suitable to true spiritual development. The traditional accounts of his life relate that he broke his prolonged fast with a meal of milk-rice offered by the woman Sujata. The effect this food had on his body and mind was extraordinary; it filled him with strength, clarity and bliss. This sudden resurgence of mental and physical energy increased not only his determination but also his ability to gain the full enlightenment that was his goal. The fact that he then went on to achieve complete liberation after only one night's meditation under the Tree of Enlightenment clearly shows that the time was ripe for him to abandon his previous ascetic practices. From a tantric point of view, these events show that the path of utilizing pleasure and desire is far more profound and effective than the path of rigid self-denial.

Later, after Buddha had become well-known as a highly realized teacher capable of guiding all different types of people to fulfilment, a king requested to be shown a path of spiritual development suitable for someone with important social obligations. 'As a king I have the responsibility of taking care of my subjects,' he explained, 'and it would be wrong for me to abandon them. I cannot do as you did: give everything away, go into the jungle and follow the ascetic life. What I need is a way of using the royal life itself as a path to spiritual fulfilment. Therefore, if you have a method for transforming my everyday actions as a king into a spiritual path, please teach it to me.' Buddha replied that he did, in fact, have such a method: the practice of tantra. 'With this method you can continue to discharge your responsibilities,' he explained, 'and need not give up any of your royal pleasures.' He told the king that he could, in fact, enjoy himself as much as possible and still be progressing towards enlightenment.

The teaching that Buddha gave the king was the Kalachakra (Cycle of Time) Tantra, and the lineages of this and many other tantric teachings have remained unbroken and powerful up to the present day. Countless Indians and Tibetans have achieved full enlightenment by following these methods and there is absolutely no reason why Westerners cannot benefit in the same way.

FOLLOWING THE PATH TODAY

Tantra is particularly well-suited to the Western mentality; being the quickest of all paths it should appeal strongly to the West's love of instant results. Furthermore, the path of tantra is essentially one of transformation, and the principle of transformation of energy — on a material level at least — is well understood in the West. Finally, while the great explosion of desirous energy in this century is considered to be a serious obstacle to most spiritual paths, it is actually helpful for the practice of tantra where desire is the fuel propelling us to our highest destination. Perhaps only a path like tantra, with its emphasis on direct experience rather than blind acceptance, can rouse us out of our self-destructive patterns and give us the opportunity to fulfil ourselves completely.

However, if we are to derive real value from this path we have to be clear about certain important points. First of all, our motivation for practising tantra must be as pure as possible. This point will be discussed at greater length later (see Chapter 6); for now it is enough to say that there is absolutely no way for us to reap the immeasurable benefits of tantra if our motivation is centred on our own welfare alone. The only type of person for whom tantra can work is someone who is primarily concerned with benefiting others and sees the tantric path as the quickest and most powerful way of accomplishing this altruistic aim.

Secondly, we must have the patience and self-discipline to engage in the practices in a well-ordered manner. To think, as many people do, 'Since tantra is the highest path, it is not necessary for me to bother about the preliminary practices' and then jump into the most advanced teachings is both foolish and arrogant; it is also very dangerous. Anyone who has such an impatient and unrealistic attitude is completely unqualified to receive instruction in tantra.

Finally, it is very important to be able to differentiate clearly between the essence of tantra and the cultural forms in which it is currently wrapped. What I mean by this is that there is no benefit in a Westerner's pretending to look or act like a Tibetan, or any other Oriental for that matter. Learning to say prayers in a foreign language, for instance, is not in itself the way to fulfil our highest human potential; there is nothing of transcending value to be gained from substituting one set of cultural conventions for another. People whose practice remains on this superficial level end up with nothing but confusion, not knowing who they are or what they should do. Of course, during this time of transition when the tantric teachings are moving from the East to the West, there is a lot to be gained from the study of the Tibetan language and so forth. But my point is that we should always bear in mind that tantra is something far deeper than language or custom. What tantra has to teach us is a way of breaking free from *all* the conditioning that limits our understanding of who we are and what we can become. If we approach these powerful teachings with clear-sighted intelligence and a strong determination to extract their essence, we can definitely bring to our life the wholeness and inner satisfaction that we all seek.

Four-Armed Chenrezig

3 Pleasure, Disappointment and Fulfilment

TANTRA AND ENJOYMENT

The function of tantra is to transform all pleasures into the transcendental experience of deep penetrative awareness. Instead of advocating separation from worldly pleasures the way many other traditions do, tantra emphasizes that it is much more effective for human beings to enjoy themselves and channel the energy of their enjoyments into a quick and powerful path to fulfilment and enlightenment. This is the most skilful way of using our precious human potential.

Through its methods of profound transformation, tantra demonstrates that as human beings we have the capacity to enjoy limitless, blissful happiness while at the same time remaining free of the delusions that normally contaminate our pursuit of pleasure. Contrary to what some people might believe, there is nothing wrong with having pleasures and enjoyments. What *is* wrong is the confused way we grasp onto these pleasures, turning them from a source of happiness into a source of pain and dissatisfaction. It is such grasping and attachment that is the problem, not the pleasures themselves. Therefore, if we could free ourselves from this habitual grasping, we could enjoy ourselves as much as we want without any of the difficulties that usually accompany our ordinary compulsive search for pleasure.

With the proper understanding of transformation, whatever we do, twenty-four hours a day, can bring us closer to our goal of totality and self-fulfilment. All our actions — walking, eating and even urinating! — can be brought into our spiritual path. Even our sleep, which is usually spent in the darkness of unconsciousness or in the chaos of dreams, can be turned into the clear light experience of subtle, penetrating wisdom.

Perhaps all this sounds impossible. Certainly other more gradual spiritual approaches, including those of the sutra path of Buddhism itself, stress that desire, jealousy and the other delusions of our daily life are always impure and should be treated as poisons. We are constantly reminded of their dangerous effects and are instructed to avoid their influence as much as possible. But, as has been pointed out already, tantra takes a different approach. Although it also insists that delusions such as desirous attachment are the source of our dissatisfaction and suffering and therefore must be overcome, it teaches skilful ways of using the energy of these delusions to deepen our awareness and speed our spiritual progress. Just as those with skill can take poisonous plants and turn them into powerful medicine, so too can the skilful and well-trained tantric practitioner manipulate the energy of desire and even anger to advantage. This is definitely possible.

IMAGES OF WHOLENESS

Tantra not only teaches us how to take advantage of our ordinary pleasurable experiences, it also shows us how to activate a deeper, more intense and ultimately more satisfying experience of bliss than is ordinarily available through our physical senses.

At present our search for pleasure is habitually directed outwards towards external objects of our desire. When we cannot find, or hold onto, these desired objects, we become frustrated and unhappy. For example, many of us are looking for the man or the woman of our dreams, someone who will be the source of limitless happiness for us, yet no matter how many boyfriends or girlfriends we might collect, these dreams remain unfulfilled.

What we do not realize is that within each one of us is an unlimited source of both male and female energy. So many of our problems arise because we are either ignorant of, or we suppress, what we have within us. Men try to hide their female side and women are afraid of expressing their male energy. As a result we always feel cut off from something we need. We do not feel whole and therefore turn expectantly towards other people for the qualities missing in ourselves in the hope of gaining some sense of completeness. As a result, much of our behaviour becomes contaminated by insecurity and possessiveness. In fact, *all* the problems in the world, from one person's anxiety to warfare between nations, can be traced to this feeling of not being whole.

If necessary, great yogis and yoginis can spend years in solitary isolation without feeling lonely. Yet we may feel unbearably lonely if we are separated from our boyfriend or girlfriend for even one day! Why is there such a great difference between ourselves and the yogis? This has to do with our own internal male and female energies. As long as they are fragmented and unbalanced we will remain desperate for the company of others and incapable of being satisfied. If our internal male/female *mandala* were complete, however, we would never experience the pain of loneliness at all.

Tantra provides powerful methods for getting in touch with our essential wholeness. Tantric art is filled with potent symbols of the unity and completeness characteristic of our fully realized potential. The image of male and female deities in sexual embrace — taken by some early Western interpreters of Tibetan Buddhism as a sign of its degeneration — is a symbolic portrayal of the inner unification of our own male and female energies. On a deeper level, their embrace symbolizes the aim of the very highest tantric practices: generation of a most subtle and blissful state of mind that, by its very nature, is supremely suited to penetrate ultimate reality and free us from all delusion and suffering. On this level, the male figure represents the experience of great bliss while the female is the symbol of non-dual wisdom. Thus their union has nothing whatsoever to do with the gratification of the senses but rather indicates a totally integrated state of blissful wisdom that completely transcends ordinary sense desires.

For those who are ripe, merely seeing such an image can help restore the connection between the male and female aspects of their being. For this connection to be re-established, however, it is necessary to cut through the influence of the over-intellectualizing conceptual mind. It is this type of conceptualization that is largely responsible for the feeling of being alienated from our inner reality. That is one reason why symbols and images such as those used in tantric art and visualization can be so much more effective than mere words in introducing us to our essential nature.

FOUR CLASSES OF TANTRA

There are four classes or levels of buddhist tantra known respectively as action, performance, yoga and highest yoga tantra. Each class is designed for a particular type of practitioner and what differentiates one class from another is the intensity of desirous energy the practitioner is skilful enough to direct into the spiritual path. Traditionally, these differing levels of blissful energy are illustrated by examples of increasing sexual intimacy. Thus it is said that the practitioner of the lowest level of tantra is one who is able to use and transform the blissful energy that arises merely from looking at an attractive partner. On the second level, it is the energy of exchanging smiles or laughter with this partner that is transformed. On the third level, the energy used is that of holding hands while the qualified practitioner of highest yoga tantra has the skill to direct into the spiritual path the desirous energy of sexual union itself. This very powerful imagery gives us an idea of the steadily increasing range of energy that can be channeled and transformed through the practice of tantra.

The practical question is how to make the techniques of tantric transformation work for us individually. It is easy to talk in a general way about the theory and practice of tantra, about taking desire as the path to enlightenment, but such talk is of little value. What is truly important is to determine, from a close examination of our own capabilities and experiences, the way we handle desirous energy at the moment. We have to ask ourselves how much sensory pleasure we can handle without going berserk. While it is true that tantric practice can eventually arouse a subtle, penetrating state of consciousness, which by its own nature is extraordinarily blissful, this does not mean it is a good idea for us to follow our desires indiscriminately now merely because they too lead to some bliss. We have to be honest about our present limitations and realistic about our present abilities if our practice of tantra is ever to amount to anything worthwhile.

One of the biggest obstacles to true spiritual development is arrogance. This danger is particularly great in relation to the practice of tantra. We may feel that since tantra is advertized as a way of utilizing desire, all we have to do is indulge our uncontrolled appetites or increase the number of desires we already have and we will be following the path of a true practitioner. Some people do have this attitude, but it is completely mistaken. We should never forget that if wallowing in desire were the same as practising tantra, we would all be highly evolved tantric yogis and yoginis by now! Although our life has been filled with unquenchable desires for this and that, the only thing we have gained from these desires so far is more and more dissatisfaction.

Why is this so? What is it about our ordinary desires that leads inevitably to frustration and disappointment? If we don't understand this, all our talk about using desire as the path to enlightenment is nothing but a joke.

DESIRE AND DISTORTION

It is important to understand that the type of desire we ordinarily have for an attractive object distorts our perception of that object. An obvious example of this is sexual desire. To take just one instance of such distortion, consider the case of a man who has become infatuated with a particular woman (or, for that matter, one person with any other). Even if this woman is someone who would generally be considered attractive, the man's desire for her exaggerates her beauty to a ridiculous extent. The more obsessive his desire, the more unrealistic his image of her becomes. Eventually, this image comes to bear no relation whatsoever to reality. Then, instead of being attracted to the woman herself, the man has become infatuated by a projection of her that he himself has created.

This tendency to exaggerate and project is not limited to any one culture; it is a universal phenomenon. When two people look at each other through the eyes of excessive desire, each one makes up an incredible story about the other. 'Oh, such beauty! There is nothing even slightly wrong here, inside or out.' They build up a perfect myth. Because of infatuation and desire, each becomes blind to the imperfections of the other and exaggerates his or her good qualities beyond recognition. This exaggeration is just the superstitious interpretation, the projection, of the mind obsessed with desire.

To a greater or lesser extent, this tendency to exaggerate is characteristic of all our ordinary desires. We overestimate the beauty or worth of whatever it is we are attracted to and lose sight of its actual nature. We forget, for instance, that this object of our desire — whether it is a person or a thing — is changing all the time, just as we ourselves are. We act as if it will exist forever as something beautiful and desirable, something that will give us eternal joy and satisfaction. Such a conception of permanence is, of course, completely out of touch with reality and by holding onto it we are setting ourselves up for nothing but disappointment.

It is important to understand that this habit of projecting a false notion of permanence upon what we find desirable is not something we do consciously. If we are asked, 'Do you think your boyfriend — or girlfriend, or new car, or whatever — will last forever and always be beautiful?' we will immediately say, 'Of course not!' We are too familiar with the forces of change, decay, ageing and death to answer otherwise. But for most of us this understanding is merely intellectual. It is an idea that we know with our brain but is not yet a realization we feel from our heart. If we check our deep, heartfelt attitude towards what we desire, we will discover an habitual grasping for permanence that remains basically untouched by whatever intellectual understanding of the process of change we may have. Just look at the way our heart shakes with anticipation when we are caught up in strong desire for someone or something. Would we experience such intense agitation if we did not hold the unrealistic expectations that we do?

Do not misinterpret this point. I am not trying to be excessively critical, saying that all our ideas are superficial or that all our emotional reactions are perverse. I am just trying to explore a situation that people everywhere have experienced for themselves: namely that although our desires are aimed at bringing us happiness, we nevertheless remain unfulfilled and dissatisfied. If we do not understand the reason for this, any hopes we may have of using desire to gain the complete happiness of spiritual fulfilment are doomed.

THE SOURCE OF DISSATISFACTION

So where does the fault lie? Who or what is responsible for our continual failure to experience the happiness and peace we are so desperately searching for? To answer this question, let us look closely once more at the way ordinary desire works. Feeling somehow incomplete, insecure and unfulfilled, we look outside ourselves for something or someone that will make us feel whole. Either consciously or subconsciously we feel, 'If only I had such-and-such, *then* I would be happy!' With this thought as our impulse we try to possess whatever attractive object seems most likely to fulfil our desire. In the process we turn the object into an idol, overestimating its attractive qualities until it bears little resemblance to its actual nature.

In our attempt to gain possession of this overestimated object of desire, we may be either successful or unsuccessful. If we are unsuccessful in our striving — if the object remains outside our grasp — then of course we are disappointed; the more we desire the object the more distraught we become when we are unable to possess it.

But what happens when we are successful, when we do get what we want? What we end up with and what we hoped to end up with turn out to be two very different things. For what we find ourselves in possession of is not the longed-for dream image — the permanent, complete and ever-satisfying solution to our deepest problems — but something that is as imperfect, incomplete and impermanent as we are ourselves. This person or thing may indeed give us some momentary pleasure, but it can never begin to live up to the expectations we have loaded upon it. And so sooner or later we feel cheated and bitterly disappointed.

Now, to return to the original question, whom or what do we blame for our unhappiness? More often than not, we unreasonably blame the object. 'If only she were prettier ....' 'If only he treated me better....' 'If only the car were faster, or newer....' If only this, if only that. These are the dualistic considerations that fill our head when, disappointed with what we have, we wonder what we could replace it with that would guarantee us the happiness we crave. The next thing we know we are searching for a new wife, or a new husband, or a new car, placing expectations on this new object that are just as unrealistic as the expectations we had placed on what we are now discarding. In this way we continue to circle around and around, changing this and that in our life but never really getting any closer to our desired happiness and peace of mind.

THE TANTRIC SOLUTION

The tantric solution to this problem is extremely radical; it involves a complete transformation of our ordinary vision. This is the central point of the tantric approach. The same desirous energy that ordinarily propels us from one unsatisfactory situation to another is transmuted, through the alchemy of tantra, into a transcendental experience of bliss and wisdom. The practitioner focuses the penetrating brilliance of this blissful wisdom so that it cuts like a laser beam through all false projections of this and that and pierces the very heart of reality.

The various levels of confusion and conflict that now obscure our mind and prevent us from experiencing the totality of our human potential are systematically eradicated by the force of this blissful awareness. Thus the energy of desire is harnessed in such a way that, instead of increasing our dissatisfaction as it ordinarily does, it destroys the very cause of our dissatisfaction: our fundamental ignorance of the nature of reality.

In the Tibetan tantric tradition, this transformation of desirous energy is illustrated by the following analogy. There are certain insects who are said to be born from wood; that is, their life cycle begins with their hatching deep within the body of a tree. Then, as they grow they feed upon the tree, eating the very wood out of which they were born. Similarly, through the practice of tantric transformation, desire gives birth to insightful wisdom, which in turn consumes all the negativities obscuring our mind, including the desire that gave it birth.

So, we can see that the ordinary and the enlightened functions of desire are directly opposed to one another. In tantra, the experience of the bliss that arises from desire *expands* the mind so that we overcome all our limitations, whereas ordinarily the pleasure that comes from contact with desirable objects *narrows* our attention and leads to a restrictive obsession for more and better pleasure. Intoxicated by pleasurable sensations, we lose our awareness of totality and sink into a state of dull stupidity. Our mind contracts around its object and, as we grasp at it for more and more satisfaction, we become further and further removed from reality. We can almost say that under the spell of strong desire we sink into a type of unconsciousness. When we eventually wake up from this dull, dreamlike state, we find that any pleasure we might have experienced has disappeared and all that is left is the dissatisfaction we started with.

To put it another way, we can say that normally our experience of pleasure is dark, clouded by ignorance. Although there may be some momentary excitement, there is no clear mindfulness, no light. In tantric practice the idea is to unify our experience of pleasure with light. This unification is represented visually, as I mentioned, by the image of a male and a female deity embracing. This signifies the unification of the male energy of bliss and the female energy of penetrative, non-dual wisdom. Ultimately, these two have to come together for us to experience the true fulfilment of our deepest nature. Because such unity of bliss and wisdom is not our present habit we have to make a great effort to cultivate this experience of totality.

A NOTE OF CAUTION

Because the habit of falling into a state of dullness and confusion as we grasp onto pleasure is so deeply ingrained in us, it is unreasonable to imagine that we can immediately transform intensely desirous energy into pure and expansive mental clarity. Even though tantra is the quickest path to the completeness of the enlightened experience, we still must progress in stages according to our capacity, otherwise we will be taking on a burden we are not yet strong enough to carry. We then risk ending up like those poor countries who, in their efforts to modernize themselves, have taken on too much too quickly. So often the unfortunate result is that their simple and relatively balanced lives are thrown into confusion. Thus, although the intended purpose of their rapid industrialization was to bring benefit, the actual result is even greater restlessness and dissatisfaction than before. Similarly, if our practice of tantric transformation is not appropriate to our emotional level and mental capacity − if we think to take on and transform more desirous energy than we can handle − this will only lead us to a more confused state than we are in at the moment.

Manjushri

4 Overthrowing the Tyranny of Ordinary Appearances

BEYOND LIMITATIONS: SEEING ONESELF AS A DEITY

So, we can see that the energy of desire can affect us in two completely opposite ways. Through the transformative methods of tantra, this energy can be transmuted into light, blissful wisdom and thus become a potent force in our development. Ordinarily, however, this desirous energy feeds into habitual patterns of grasping and attachment, which only decrease our awareness while reinforcing our ignorance and dissatisfaction. One of the major tasks facing the spiritual seeker is to identify as precisely as possible the factors responsible for perpetuating this cycle of dissatisfaction and then to apply the most appropriate antidote to their destructiveness. Only then can best use be made of tantra's transformative powers.

According to buddhist tantra, we remain trapped within a circle of dissatisfaction because our view of reality is narrow and suffocating. We hold onto a very limited and limiting view of who we are and what we can become, with the result that our self-image remains oppressively low and negative, and we feel quite inadequate and hopeless.

As long as our opinion of ourselves is so miserable, our life will remain meaningless. Many people feel that humans are little more than monkeys and that the human mind is nothing but a series of chemical reactions and electrical impulses in the brain. Such a view reduces us to lumps of matter and dismisses any notion of a higher dimension to human existence. For people who truly believe in such a narrow view of what it means to be human, what is the purpose of remaining alive? Perhaps it is merely to experience as many sensations of pleasure as possible before we decay back to our basic nature: dust. Such a depressing outlook may account for much of the alienation in modern society.

Tantra challenges this unreasonably low opinion of human potential by showing us how to view ourselves and all others as transcendentally beautiful — as gods and goddesses in fact. One of the essential practices at all levels of tantra is to dissolve our ordinary conceptions of ourselves and then, from the empty space into which these concepts have disappeared, arise in the glorious light body of a deity: a manifestation of the essential clarity of our deepest being. The more we train to see ourselves as such a meditational deity, the less bound we will feel by life's ordinary disappointments and frustrations. This divine self-visualization empowers us to take control of our life and create for ourselves a pure environment in which our deepest nature can be expressed.

Tantric meditational deities should not be confused with what different mythologies and religions might mean when they speak of gods and goddesses. Here, the deity we choose to identify with represents the essential qualities of the fully awakened experience latent within us. To use the language of psychology, such a deity is an archetype of our own deepest nature, our most profound level of consciousness. In tantra we focus our attention upon such an archetypal image and identify with it in order to arouse the deepest, most profound aspects of our being and bring them into our present reality. It is a simple truth that if we identify ourselves as being fundamentally pure, strong and capable we will actually develop these qualities, but if we continue to think of ourselves as dull and foolish, *that* is what we will become.

To give an example of tantric transformation, we might visualize ourselves as Manjushri, a princely deity usually represented as reddish yellow in colour, holding the sword of discriminating awareness in his right hand and a text of Buddha's *Perfection of Wisdom* teachings in his left. (This we can do whether we are a man or a woman since tantric visualizations completely transcend our ordinary identification as male or female.) But such a visualized image is not, in fact, the actual Manjushri. Wisdom itself — the completely unobscured insight of a mind that has realized its full potential — is the actual Manjushri, and the purpose of seeing ourselves in the form of this particular deity is to hasten the development of the wisdom already within us. Manjushri's double-edged sword, for example, symbolizes the ability of enlightened wisdom to discriminate between what is true and what is false by cutting through misconceptions and superstitions. The more closely we identify with such a deity, having become familiar with what each of his attributes stands for, the more deeply we stimulate in our own mind the growth of the qualities he represents.

In the early stages of practice, this process of seeing oneself as a deity is largely artificial. But as we train in deity-yoga with the proper perseverance we will be able to perceive this self-generated deity with a clarity far exceeding that of our present self-image. Our mind will actually become the mind of the deity, and our ordinary sensory experiences — what we see, hear, taste and so forth — will be transformed into the blissful enjoyments of the deity. This is not a fairy tale. Such transformation has been the experience of countless tantric meditators of the past and there is no reason why, if we exert sufficient effort, we should not experience the same transcendental results.

PROBLEMS OF SELF-EMANATION

'But why should I emanate myself as Manjushri or any other deity?' you may ask. 'It is already difficult enough for me to emanate myself as a man, or as a woman. So why should I

change my appearance and put on another mask, a Manjushri mask?'

What we have to remember is that when we emanate
ourselves as Manjushri it is not to manifest as something
different from what we already are. We already have the
profound qualities of such a divine manifestation within us
at the moment. The reason we practise emanating ourselves
as a deity is so that we can more fully recognize and
cultivate these qualities, rather than remaining miserably
trapped within the limiting projections of the self-pitying
attitude: I am ugly, stupid, weak and worthless.'

You may still wonder, 'But how could Manjushri, or any
other tantric deity for that matter, be the essence of what I
already am? I don't look like any of these deities; I'm not
orange or blue or green; I don't have more than one face and
two arms the way many of them do.' Of course objections
like these will arise, but if we are ever going to put them to
rest we first have to examine very closely who we think we
actually are.

First of all, your present face is not you; your bones and
flesh are not you. Neither your blood, your muscles nor any
other part of your body are the essence of who you are. To an
extent you can say that your body is like a mechanical robot
because by itself it is powerless to function. It has to be
controlled by something else. And just as it is the computer
program that controls the robot and makes it function, it is
your mind — or consciousness, psyche, soul or whatever
you want to call it — that gives life to your body. Therefore,
if you are looking for the essence of who you are, if you
want to know what is responsible for how you live your life,
you have to look into your mind.

The next thing to realize is that from the time you were
born up until now you have manifested in many different
ways. None of us is static and unchanging. For example,
when you are filled with anger, you look like a demon while
at other times, filled with love, you look like a beautiful

angel. None of these manifestations — whether angry, peaceful, jealous, loving, compassionate, stupid or wise — arises primarily from your body, from your physical form. They all arise from the power of your consciousness, from the power of your mind. The mind has the ability to generate thousands of different emotions and attitudes, and the body just follows its lead without any choice. Despite this fact, however, we so often identify with our body rather than with our mind. It is as if we think the body were the boss instead of the mind. It is almost as if we become slaves of our body. Just turn on the television for a few minutes and it will be clear how much energy our culture devotes to serving the body and how little to cultivating the mind. No wonder things are so confused.

Putting the body before the mind in this way is not the only mistake we make. We also fail to realize that our gross physical body is not the only body we possess. More will be said about this later (see Chapter 10) but, briefly stated, within the confines of our ordinary physical form exists a subtler conscious body, so-called because it is intimately connected with deep levels of consciousness. It is from these subtler levels that the potential energy of blissful wisdom arises, an energy capable of transforming the quality of our life completely. Tantric deities symbolize the full development of this blissful wisdom energy and that is why we can say that such a deity — no matter what colour it is or how many faces it has — represents the essence of who we are and what we can become. Deity-yoga, therefore, is not involved with fantasizing the impossible. Rather, it is an extremely practical method for living up to our highest potential through systematic training and profound transformation of our human consciousness.

Although deity-yoga might seem very unfamiliar and impractical at first, we can get a glimpse of how effective it is by thinking of similar techniques that have already demonstrated their value even to the sceptical West. For instance, there are many documented cases where people have cured themselves of cancer and other serious illnesses solely through the process of creative visualization. Instead of holding onto the view: 'My body is filled with cancer and I am dying,' these people see themselves as whole and healthy. The image of being diseased is released from the mind and replaced by an image of radiance and vitality. On many occasions this approach has proven effective even after doctors have given up all hope.

The health of body and mind is primarily a question of our self-image. Those people who think badly of themselves, for whatever reasons, become and then remain miserable, while those who can recognize and draw on their inner resources can overcome even the most difficult situations. Deity-yoga is one of the most profound ways of lifting our self-image, and that is why tantra is such a quick and powerful method for achieving the fulfilment of our tremendous potential.

The biggest obstacle standing in the way of our successful transformation into such a deity is our persistent belief in ordinary appearances. As long as we maintain the ordinary vision we have of ourselves, there is no space for seeing ourselves as an enlightened being. We cannot truly see ourselves as possessing a deity's transparent body of light if we continue to identify so strongly with our gross physical form. And we will never be able to contact the essentially pure nature of our own being if we continue to think that our mind's fundamental nature is nothing but the delusions and gross conceptions that pass through it.

Therefore, if we truly wish to achieve the satisfaction of complete self-fulfilment, we must find a way to break free from the tyranny of ordinary appearances and conceptions. We must gain a heartfelt appreciation of how disastrous it is to continue relating to our body and our mind, and therefore our self-image, in the gross and limiting ways we do now. We need to understand that our naive acceptance of

ordinary appearances only makes us more and more confused, insecure and dissatisfied.

Any tendency we have towards indecision and fear is a
symptom of our dualistic mind, the mind that churns out a
seemingly endless succession of contradictory thoughts. 'I
hope I look good but I'm afraid I look bad.' It also demonstrates how superficial the judgements we make about ourselves usually are. After all, physical appearance is *not* a true
measure of the actual worth of any man or woman. Nevertheless, slight physical imperfections, whether real or imagined, are enough to cause us great anxiety. There are even
people who feel so ugly, so utterly worthless, so full of self-
loathing, that they starve themselves to death. This is an
extreme example, but I think most of us put ourselves down
and make ourselves miserable for one reason or another.

THE MIND DISTRACTED OUTWARDS

It sometimes seems that our mind is running in every
direction at once, turning to this and that in a desperate
search. But for what? We are looking for an unnamed
something that will satisfy our longing for stability and
security. We pass from one thing to another hoping that the
next experience will contain whatever it is we are looking
for. As a result our mind is constantly distracted. It is
difficult to focus all our attention on what we are doing
because part of our mind is already dissatisfied and has
begun to search for that illusive something else. Even when
we are doing something that we enjoy we lose our concentration so easily. Thus not only do we fail to discover a
higher meaning and purpose to our life, we are often
unsuccessful in our mundane affairs as well.

The inevitable result of our limited self-conception −
limited by our unquestioning belief in ordinary appearances − is our tendency to look outside ourselves for the

answer to our problems. Having grown accustomed to seeing ourselves as incomplete or lacking in some fundamental way, it does not cross our mind to look towards our own inner resources, our inner strength, for a solution to our difficulties. Instead, we think that something in the outer environment, if possessed somehow, will give us what we want. The futility of this approach, however, should be obvious to us all. What person or thing could we possibly make our own so that this search for security might come to an end? Neither the most beautiful woman in the world, the most handsome man, the most fashionable clothes, the most precious jewel, nor the most ingenious new idea has the power to quench our desires as long as we remain incomplete inside. As long as we think that a refuge from life's difficulties can be found outside ourselves, there is no way that we can experience true peace of mind. Certainly the possession of wealth and power is no solution. The high rate of alcoholism, divorce and suicide in the so-called developed nations of the world shows that mere material possessions do not satisfy restlessness.

Even if we turn away from material objects and towards some higher spiritual reality for a solution to our problems, our limiting self-conceptions can still severely restrict whatever benefits we may gain. It is common for people who take a religious path to feel that there is an unbridgable gap between themselves, stranded down here in the mud, and some higher being way up in the sky somewhere. The lower our opinion of our own potential, the more pitiful are the prayers that we make. We may cry, 'Please save me, God!' 'Please help me, Buddha!' but as long as we remain wrapped in our own self-pity it is questionable how much benefit we can receive.

THE CHALLENGE OF EXPLORING INNER SPACE

The tantric technique of identifying ourselves as a deity is a direct opponent to this self-pitying attitude. The more we can identify ourselves as having a body and mind of pure clear light, the more we open ourselves up to the beneficial forces existing inside and outside ourselves. We have already mentioned how, through creative visualization, we can call upon inborn forces of healing and cure ourselves of even the most dreadful diseases. As this example shows, our body and mind are dependent upon one another and, of the two, it is our mind that is the primary shaper of our experience. If the mental image we have of ourselves is positive, then our actions are naturally filled with self-confidence, and the impression we make upon others is one of strength and vitality. On the other hand, if we have a low opinion of ourselves, we appear weak and ineffective, attract many problems and easily fall victim to accident and disease.

Over and over again our experiences prove that it is our mental outlook that is fundamentally responsible for whether we are successful or unsuccessful, healthy or ill, attractive or ugly, happy or depressed. Nevertheless, when we face difficulties in our life we habitually look outside ourselves for a solution. Instead of dealing directly with our mind itself and developing an attitude that will transform our experiences for the better, we take a much more superficial approach and try to manipulate our outer circumstances in an attempt to solve our problems. But this never brings lasting satisfaction. It does not matter how many external aspects of our life we change; if these changes are not accompanied by a deep mental transformation, they can only be successful momentarily. Sooner or later our problems will reassert themselves and we will be as uncomfortable and dissatisfied as before.

Although we all have a fundamentally pure nature, it is not easy to get in touch with it. The gross way our mind ordinarily functions drowns out this deeper, more subtle vibration to such an extent that we generally remain unaware of its existence. If we truly want to connect with this subtle essence, we need to quiet all distractions and loosen the hold our ordinary appearances and conceptions have on us. In other words we need to create space, space in which our essentially pure nature can function uninterruptedly. Then, when we employ the tantric techniques of visualizing ourselves as a deity, we will not be pretending. Rather, we will be bringing to the surface the inner, divine qualities that have always existed within the depths of our being.

The methods for creating this necessary space are contained in the various prerequisites for the practice of tantra. If we attempt to use the extremely powerful transformational energies of tantra without first training in these prerequisites, or preliminaries, there is no way our practice will be successful. Instead, we may even do great harm to ourselves. A powerful jet plane may be the fastest way of getting from one place to another, but if someone without any training is put into the pilot seat the result will be nothing but disaster. Similarly, although tantra is the speediest vehicle for reaching complete fulfilment, practising its methods without first preparing our body and mind would be extremely reckless, showing deep ignorance of the entire purpose of tantra.

5 Emerging from Dissatisfaction

The major prerequisites for the practice of tantra — commonly called the three principal aspects of the sutra vehicle to enlightenment — are renunciation, the dedicated heart of *bodhicitta*, and the correct view of emptiness. Here, to emphasize that the cultivation of these three states of mind creates the space in which tantric transformation can take place, we discuss them under the chapter headings *emerging*, *opening* and *dissolving*.

First comes renunciation: the mind emerging from its ordinary, limiting preoccupations and taking an interest instead in realizing its unlimited, completely liberated potential.

WHAT IS RENUNCIATION?

Some of the preliminary methods for making space within our mind have been mentioned already. For example, tantra can only be practised effectively once we have become disillusioned with our ordinary way of grasping at sensory desires. We must have a deep, heartfelt understanding that such grasping never leads to satisfaction but only to pain and disappointment. If we fail to see how our ordinary attachment to pleasure binds us tightly to the wheel of repeated disappointment (*samsara*), we will make the same mistakes with tantra that we have been making in our ordinary pursuits of happiness. Whenever we experience a blissful sensation as a result of our practice, we will grasp at it as something self-existent and definitely capable of giving us endless enjoyment. Like a spider waiting for a fly, we will pounce greedily onto whatever attractive experience comes along. Trying to squeeze pleasure out of things in this way is completely deluded and as long as we have such an unrealistic attitude we will never know true satisfaction. If we do not let go of this grasping attitude we will unintentionally turn tantra into yet another meaningless journey around in circles.

So, first of all, we need to develop a certain amount of renunciation. Because renunciation is often confused with the fearful, rejecting state of mind I criticized earlier, perhaps I will start by describing what renunciation is *not*.

If a situation is difficult, we can renounce it by giving it up or avoiding it; this may be called renunciation but it is not the renunciation of samsara. Or perhaps our heart is broken because we fought with our friend, so we move to another city to escape further pain. Again, this is not re- nunciation. Or perhaps we cannot cope with society any longer so we run away into the bush declaring, 'I renounce worldly life completely!' By living like an animal without any of the conveniences of civilization we are certainly renouncing something, but this is still not true renunciation.

We may think that renunciation has something to do with religious observance, that by studying spiritual teachings and practising meditation we are a true renunciate. But this is not necessarily so. If someone criticizes what we are doing — 'You are just on a weird Eastern trip!' — and we get upset, this shows we have not developed renunciation at all. In- stead, it is a sign that we are holding onto our religion as we would any ordinary sense object. In other words, by our grasping attitude we have turned a spiritual practice into yet another form of ordinary attachment.

What the development of true renunciation implies is that we no longer rely on sensory pleasures for our ultimate happiness; we see the futility of expecting deep satisfaction from such limited, transitory phenomena. It is important to understand this point clearly. Renunciation is *not* the same as giving up pleasure or denying ourselves happiness. It means giving up our unreal expectations about ordinary pleasures. These expectations themselves are what turn pleasure into pain. It cannot be said too often that there is nothing wrong with pleasure. It is our grasping, exaggerating, distorting and polluting attitude towards pleasure that must be abandoned.

DEVELOPING DETACHMENT

The Tibetan term generally translated as 'renunciation' has the literal meaning of 'definite emergence.' It indicates a deep, heartfelt decision definitely to emerge from the repeated frustrations and disappointments of ordinary life. Simply stated, renunciation is the feeling of being so completely fed up with our recurring problems that we are finally ready to turn away from our attachments to this and that and begin searching for another way to make our life satisfying and meaningful. Thus the cultivation of renunciation, or definite emergence, involves detaching ourselves from those sticky habits of attachment that hold us back from experiencing our fullest human potential.

There are certain times during our life (as will be discussed in Chapter 10) when our senses automatically withdraw from their objects and we experience what could be called a natural detachment, or a natural renunciation. At such times there is nothing for us to grasp onto and nothing for us to be attached to. In such a state, even the most attractive sensory object is powerless to magnetize and divert our mind. But generally we are anything but detached when it comes to the objects of our experience. We are continually attracted to and hypnotized by a never-ending stream of sense impressions and forever on the look-out for something new and different to excite and interest us. If we own a car, that is not good enough: we need two. And when we have two, it is still not good enough: we need a boat. Even the boat is not enough: we need a bigger one. And so it goes on and on to infinity. This is dissatisfaction, the very opposite of the truly renounced, or emerging, mind.

Somehow we need to learn to be natural, to be naturally detached from material objects, from our grasping after this and that. I am not saying this because, as a backward Tibetan, I am jealous of wealthy Westerners. Nor am I saying that you are bad because you remain rich while others are poor. I am merely trying to answer the question: 'Why are we dissatisfied?'

We can always find some external cause to blame for our dissatisfaction — 'There is not enough of this, not enough of that' — but this is never the real reason for our restlessness and disappointment. What is missing is *inside* and this is what we all have to recognize. Satisfaction is *not* dependent on material objects; it is something that comes from simplicity, inner simplicity.

When I talk of being detached what I mean is to be simpler, more easy-going. Detachment does not mean totally renouncing everything. It means that you loosen your grip and be more relaxed. There are a lot of pleasures available in the world, but as long as you are uptight and anxious, fearfully holding onto your money and possessions, your wealth will only make you more and more unhappy. If you do not know how to relax and be satisfied with what you have, if you do not know how to appreciate the natural beauty of your environment, if you do not know how to be simple, then even if you were to possess all the money in the world you would still be miserable.

Renunciation, then, does not mean that we should give up our pleasure. Far from it! The whole philosophy of Buddhism in general and of tantra in particular is that, as human beings with virtually unlimited potential, we should aim for the highest pleasure possible. What true renunciation is based on is the realization that our ordinary pleasures are second rate. They are inconsequential when compared with the extraordinary bliss to be had from awakening the energies latent within us and fulfilling our deepest potential.

Not only are these ordinary pleasures second rate, but our grasping at them prevents us from experiencing the superior happiness of full self-realization. Our grasping, squeezing attitude is an intoxicant that dulls our natural clarity. We become more and more deeply enmeshed in the world of ordinary appearances and more and more removed from our essential nature. To develop renunciation means to realize how our ordinary reliance on pleasure is preventing us from tasting this higher, more complete happiness.

With the proper development of renunciation we give ourselves a break from our usual compulsive and constricting reliance on sense pleasures. The more we understand that these pleasures are not capable of giving us the lasting happiness we desire, the more we relax our expectations and become realistic. Instead of being uptight, from either craving after pleasure or rejecting it guiltily, we feel more at ease. Unpleasant circumstances cease to bother us so much. And if we experience something pleasant we accept it comfortably, taking what enjoyment it has to give without demanding or expecting anything more from it. We can be relaxed in this way not only because we understand that these pleasures are transitory, but because our sights are set on an even higher form of happiness: the fulfilment of our essential nature. With this transcendental goal in mind we do not become overly excited by the fleeting pleasures we experience nor do we become depressed when things are going badly. In other words, instead of taking refuge in sensory objects as the solution to our dissatisfaction, we place our reliance on our own inner potential.

GIVING UP FALSE REFUGE

The phrase 'taking refuge' is borrowed from its traditional context — the often-repeated buddhist declaration of faith in the teachers, teachings and spiritual community: 'I take refuge in the buddhas, I take refuge in the *dharma*, I take refuge in the *sangha*' — to make the point that taking refuge in momentary, transitory pleasures is something we are doing all the time with an almost religious fervour and conviction. For example, one day we may think, 'Oh, I am so depressed; I think I'll go to the beach,' so we drive to the ocean, jump into the water, play around like fish and then lie down to fry in the sun. When this becomes boring, we think, 'Now I am hungry; where is the refreshment stand?' Then we stuff ourselves with as much junk food as possible, hoping to find some satisfaction in the ice cream, popcorn, coke and chocolate we are devouring. We take refuge in these things as a way out of our depression and boredom, only to end up fat and sunburnt.

When Buddhism speaks of taking refuge it is emphasizing the importance of breaking out of this desperate, unfulfilling search for satisfaction. Taking true refuge involves a changing of our attitude; it comes from seeing the ultimate worthlessness of the transitory phenomena we are ordinarily attracted to. When we see clearly the unsatisfactory character of the things we have been chasing after, our compulsive striving for them will automatically diminish and the driving force of our grasping will subside. We cease to be tossed this way and that by the changing fortunes of our life and gain the space to begin tapping our inner potential.

6   *Opening the Heart*

SELFISHNESS OR DEDICATION TO OTHERS?

So far the spiritual path has been described in terms of our own fulfilment. As we realize that our accustomed way of relating to desirable objects has been keeping us trapped in a circle of perpetual dissatisfaction, we become more and more motivated to activate a deeper level of our being. Our purpose is to experience a type of peace and happiness that is stable and reliable, unruffled by changing circumstances and uninfluenced by the passage of time. But even this higher aspiration to win release from the frustrating cycle of desire and dissatisfaction is still incomplete. Why? Because it is primarily concerned with only our own welfare.

Before, perhaps, our desires were limited to the possession of sensory objects, while now — through the development of some renunciation — they are directed towards the realization of our deepest potential. But the emphasis still remains, '*I* want this, *I* don't want that.'

This narrow concern for our own happiness and our own liberation makes it impossible for us to realize the vast potential of our human mind and heart. Such self-centred concern values the welfare of just one being — myself — over the welfare of the countless others who share life's problems with us. This extremely restricted view inevitably causes our heart to close. Then, even if we do not say so consciously, it is as if we feel, 'I am the most important person in the world. The problems that others have are of no concern to me; it is only my own happiness that counts.'

As long as we remain so tightly focused upon our own happiness, whether temporal or ultimate, we will never experience the expansiveness of a truly open heart. The only way to achieve the total vision of complete enlightenment is to free ourselves from the restrictions of this narrow, self-cherishing attitude. In the teachings of all the highly evolved men and women of the past it is clearly stated that this narrow, self-cherishing habit of mind brings us nothing but spiritual suffocation. If we truly wish to fulfil our highest potential — or even if we only want to achieve a certain mundane satisfaction in our daily life — then we must overcome this self-cherishing and dedicate ourselves as fully as possible to the welfare of others. This is the only way to achieve a completely opened heart, the only way to experience lasting happiness.

Dedication simply means that, having created a certain atmosphere of positive energy within yourself, you determine to share this happiness with others as much as possible. According to buddhist psychology, if you do not have a dedicated attitude to some extent, you will never be totally satisfied. Instead, you will remain bored and lonely. As the Panchen Lama says in his tantric text entitled *Offering to the Spiritual Master*, 'Self-cherishing is the cause of all misery and dissatisfaction, while holding all mother sentient beings dearer than oneself is the foundation of all realizations and knowledge. Therefore, inspire me to change my self-cherishing into concern for all others.' This is not some complex philosophical theory but a very simple statement. To see whether or not our self-cherishing is the cause of all our confusion and frustration all we have to do is look at our own life's experiences.

The Panchen Lama goes on to suggest that we take a good look at what Shakyamuni Buddha did with his life. He gave up all his self-attachment, dedicated himself completely to the welfare of others and as a result attained the unsurpassed bliss of complete enlightenment. Then look at us. We are obsessed with me, me, me — but the only thing we have gained is unending misery and disappointment. This is a very simple, straightforward comparison and we do not need to rely on the authority of the Panchen Lama or anyone else to see the truth it is pointing to. All the evidence we need is available in our own life and in the lives of others. Check up carefully and it will become clear that narrow selfishness always leads to disappointment and equally clear that open-hearted dedication to others brings about happiness and a sense of well-being.

THE OPEN-HEARTED BODHICITTA MOTIVATION

We have already seen how our habitual attachment to sense objects prevents us from experiencing the happiness and satisfaction we all want. If we are sincerely intent on achieving the highest human pleasure, therefore, we must give our mind space by developing an attitude of renunciation. That is, we must renounce our habitual grasping after pleasure so that we can experience *true* pleasure. Similarly, as long as we remain obsessively concerned with our own happiness alone, we will never experience the supreme happiness of a fully enlightened mind. In other words, if we wish to reach the highest possible destination we must cultivate the highest possible motivation for following the spiritual path.

In buddhist terminology this supreme motivation is known as *bodhicitta*. It is the impulse to achieve full enlightenment (*bodhi*, or buddhahood) in order to be of the most benefit to others. Only through dedicating ourselves to working for the happiness of all beings — in other words only by cultivating the open heart of bodhicitta — can we ever experience supreme happiness ourselves.

The dedicated attitude of bodhicitta is the powerful energy capable of transforming our mind completely. This can be shown to be true through our own experience; it is not something we have to believe in with blind faith. When you have developed bodhicitta in your heart all the good things in life are magnetically attracted to you and effortlessly pour down upon you like rain. At present, because our heart is filled with self-cherishing thoughts, all we seem to attract is misfortune. But with bodhicitta we automatically attract good friends, good food, good everything.

As the Dalai Lama has said, if you are going to be selfish, at least be *wisely* selfish. What he means by this peculiar-sounding advice is that in a way bodhicitta is like a huge selfish attitude: when you dedicate yourself to others with loving-kindness, you get back far more happiness than you could ever experience otherwise. Ordinarily, we get so little happiness, and it is easily lost. So if we want to be as happy as possible, the only thing to do is to dedicate ourselves wholeheartedly to the welfare of others.

LIBERATION FROM SELF-CHERISHING

We should not think that bodhicitta is a 'religious' attitude, something that we have to believe in and accept on faith alone. This supremely compassionate outlook is a direct result of clear insight into our own essential reality and the reality of others. Whenever we are concerned just with ourselves, our problems seem insurmountable. Preoccupied with thoughts of me, our mind is filled with worry and anxiety. 'Maybe I'm not good-looking enough,' 'Maybe others won't like me,' 'I wonder if I will succeed.' And so on. Everything related to this 'I' becomes a problem, a worry, a threat to our well-being and security.

The only way to break free from this neurotic obsession with ourselves is by opening our hearts to others. When we are truly concerned with the welfare of someone else we automatically cease to be so concerned with our own problems, at least for a while. And as compassion for others replaces pity for ourselves, we discover hidden treasures of strength and wisdom within us. It can be said that merely possessing this compassionate bodhicitta is a type of enlightened experience. As we create this open space in our consciousness, we take on a much more universal character. Instead of being confined in our own petty reality, we move into the larger sphere of universal concern. This automatically liberates us from most of our problems.

So often we make such a fuss of insignificant events in our life that we turn minor difficulties into major problems. As we develop the universal view of bodhicitta, however, these small concerns become unimportant and no longer bother us. As this burden of self-concern drops from our shoulders, we experience a small taste of the complete freedom that comes with full spiritual fulfilment. Experiences like this are encouraging because they demonstrate so convincingly the practical, day-to-day value of training and transforming our mind.

MISCONCEPTIONS ABOUT BODHICITTA

When some people first hear about bodhicitta they confuse it with a sentimental, highly emotional state of mind: 'Oh how I want people to be happy! I cannot stand to think of their suffering.' They feel so overwhelmed by the needs of others that their mind becomes depressed. But true bodhicitta is not at all like this; it has nothing to do with such an upset and paralyzed state of mind. Instead, it is clear and easy going, possessing a calm wisdom as well as a deeply felt compassion. It is an attitude of opening our heart completely and leaving it open as much as we can.

There is another mistaken idea that many people have when they first hear teachings on bodhicitta. Because it is necessary to develop our own inner potential to the full in order to benefit others in the deepest, most complete way, they believe that they cannot do *anything* to help others until they finally become a buddha. 'First I must study hard for many years,' they think, 'and then I can begin the practice of mental training. After a long time I might develop renunciation and bodhicitta and then, some time in the distant future when I become enlightened, I can begin to benefit others.

Such an attitude is completely mistaken; we are only burdening ourselves with a rigid conception of how our spiritual life can develop. It is just another restraint, another fantasy. If we believe strongly in such a fixed program for our life, before we know it our death will come and we won't even have started!

The fact is, while we are cultivating love, compassion, wisdom and all the other insights that lead to enlightenment, we can be helping others continuously. First of all, merely by living a simple life with a heart dedicated to overcoming self-cherishing, we automatically benefit others. And secondly, each stage of spiritual development, from the first to the last, has its own power and ability; depending on which level we have reached, we can help others to that extent. To be realistic, we should help others to the limit of our present capacity. The thought that we cannot do anything until we are enlightened is in fact egotistic and ignorant and reflects a basic misunderstanding of what spiritual training is all about.

This misunderstanding is related to an attitude we have had throughout our lives. At school, for instance, we thought, 'I must study these boring subjects now so that eventually I can pass my examinations, receive my degree, get a good job, make a lot of money, and *then* I will be happy.' All this emphasis on the future − '*When* I have enough money,' '*When* I own my own home,' '*When* I retire' − is easily transferred to our spiritual practice: '*When* I have finished practising,' '*When* I am enlightened.' But to think in this way is quite deluded. This dream fantasy of an unreal future makes our present actions unrealistic as well.

It is important to understand that true practice is something we do from moment to moment, from day to day. We do whatever we can, with whatever wisdom we have, and dedicate it all to the benefit of others. We just live our life simply, to the best of our ability. This in itself will be of enormous benefit to others; we don't need to wait until we are buddhas before we can begin to act.

DEVELOPING EQUANIMITY: THE FOUNDATION FOR UNIVERSAL COMPASSION

If you have a clear and simple understanding of the philosophy and psychology of bodhicitta and try to act accordingly in everyday life, experimenting with this open-hearted dedication to others in all your actions, that is a sufficient spiritual practice. That is good enough. Of course, the development of the actual bodhicitta — the state of mind in which we are automatically more concerned for others than we are for ourselves — is a profound realization, and we have a long way to go before we achieve it. We do not develop a completely opened heart merely by wishing for it; there is a long and gradual training to be engaged in.

In my mind, one of the beauties of Buddhism is that it offers us a practical training for our mind. It does not say, 'Bodhicitta is fantastic because Buddha said so!' Instead, it gives us the methods for developing such an attitude and we can then see for ourselves whether it works or not, whether it is fantastic or not.

According to these methods, the first thing we need is a sense of equanimity, or equilibrium. Just as level ground is the basis on which you build a house, so too is equanimity — an unbiased attitude towards all other beings — the foundation for cultivating bodhicitta. The experience of past meditators is that when you have achieved such equilibrium, you can cultivate bodhicitta quickly and easily. However, because our habit of discriminating sharply between friends, enemies and strangers is very deeply rooted within us, such even-mindedness is not easy to achieve. With our tremendous grasping desire we become attached to and cling to our dear friends, with aversion and hatred we reject those we do not like, and with indifference we turn a blind eye to the countless people who appear to be neither helpful nor harmful to us. As long as our mind is under the control of such attachment, aversion and indifference, we will never be able to cultivate the precious bodhicitta in our heart.

Equanimity is not an intellectual concept; it is not just another thought or idea to be played around with in your head. Rather, it is a state of mind, a specific quality of consciousness or awareness to be attained through constant familiarity. For this to happen you have to exert a great deal of effort. In other words, you have to train your mind and transform your basic attitude towards others. For example, when I first encounter a group of new people at a meditation course, say, I feel the same towards each of them. I have not met any of them before — they seem to have suddenly popped up like mushrooms — and I have not had time to develop attachment or aversion towards any of them. They all seem to be equal to me. If I take this unbiased feeling of equality that I have towards these new, unknown people and apply it both to my dear friends to whom I am attached and to my enemies and critics whom I dislike, I can start to develop true equanimity towards everyone.

There is a detailed meditation technique for the full cultivation of such equilibrium. In brief, you imagine yourself surrounded by three people: your dearest friend, your worst enemy and a total stranger. One way is to visualize your friend behind you and the enemy and stranger in front with all other beings in human form massed around you. Having surrounded yourself in this way, you carefully examine the feelings you have towards each of the three people and analyze why you have categorized them as you have.

When you ask yourself, 'Why do I feel close to just one of these people and not to the others?' you will probably discover that your reasons are very superficial, based on a few selected events. For example, perhaps you call the first person a friend because whenever you think of her you remember instances of her kindness or affection. And the second person appears to be your enemy because you remember some particularly nasty things he has done or said to you. As for the third person, the reason you call him a stranger is that you have no memory of his having ever helped or harmed you.

Your reasons for these different reactions are in fact arbitrary. If you search your memory honestly you are certain to find many instances when the three people you are thinking about did not fit comfortably into the categories you have so rigidly placed them. You may very well recall times when the enemy you now despise so much acted kindly towards you, when the friend you now care for so much provoked anger from you, and even when the person you are now indifferent to once meant a great deal to you. If you really think about this there is no way you can continue to see these people in the highly prejudicial way you do now. And when you reflect that each living being has, over beginningless past lifetimes, done the same kind and unkind things to you as the friend and enemy of this life, you will come to see that *all* are equal in having been friend, enemy and stranger to you over and over again.

By training your mind in this way, your feelings of attachment to your friend, aversion to your enemy and indifference to the stranger will begin to subside. This is the sign that you are beginning to experience a measure of equilibrium. Hold onto this feeling, and eventually, with practice, it will become an integral part of your mind.

Meditating on equilibrium is the best way of producing good mental health. Instead of paying a hundred dollars an hour to a therapist, meditate on equilibrium! Close your eyes and ignore all physical sensations. Abandon the five sense perceptions and allow yourself to sink deeply into intensive awareness of your mind's experience of equilibrium. You will definitely become more balanced, open and peaceful. After even ten minutes of this type of meditation you will come out into a different world.

There is a common misconception about the development of equilibrium. Some people think that it means becoming indifferent to everyone. They are afraid that if they lessen their attachment to their family and friends, their love and affection will disappear. But there is no need to worry. With true equilibrum there is no way we can close our heart to anyone.

The more we train ourselves to see the basic equality of everyone − having overcome our habitual tendency to stick them rigidly into categories of friend, enemy and stranger − the more our heart will open, increasing immeasurably our capacity for love. By freeing ourselves from prejudicial views we will be able to appreciate fully that everyone, without exception, wants and deserves to be happy and wishes to avoid even the slightest suffering. Therefore, from the basis of equilibrium we will be able to cultivate universal love, compassion and eventually the full realization of bodhicitta: the open heart dedicated totally to the ultimate benefit of all.

BODHICITTA IS NECESSARY FOR PRACTISING TANTRA

As a prerequisite for the successful practice of tantra, the development of bodhicitta is absolutely necessary. It has been said by all masters that to be properly qualified to practise tantra, we must possess a very strong bodhicitta motivation. Truly qualified tantric practitioners wish to follow the speediest path to enlightenment, not with the desire to gain quick liberation, but because they have unbearable compassion for others. They realize that the longer it takes them to achieve enlightenment, the longer everyone who needs help will have to wait. The lightning vehicle of tantra is therefore intended for those who wish to help others as much as possible, as quickly as possible.

Although it is true that bodhicitta is the most important prerequisite for tantric practice, in fact, it is more accurate to say that the opposite is true: that the purpose for practising tantra is to enhance the scope of one's bodhicitta.

There are so many tantric deities — Avalokiteshvara, Manjushri, Tara and the rest — into whose practice you can be initiated; there are so many deities you can meditate upon. But what are all these deities for? What is the purpose of all these practices? It is nothing other than developing and expanding the dedicated heart of bodhicitta. There is really no other reason for all these deities. In fact, all tantric meditations without exception are for the sole purpose of developing strong bodhicitta.

Take the practice of thousand-armed Avalokiteshvara, for example. The whole reason for having your consciousness manifest as a divine light-being with one thousand arms is so that you can lend a hand to one thousand suffering beings. What other reason could you have for wanting so many arms? And, if you do not feel comfortable manifesting in this way, you can always relate your meditation to your own culture and manifest your inner being as Jesus, Saint Francis, Kwan Yin or any other holy being.

What we have to understand is that Avalokiteshvara and Jesus, for example, are exactly the same; the essential nature of each is complete selfless devotion in the service of others. Therefore, when we try to be like them, through the practice of tantra, prayer or any other method, it is only to be able to serve others in a similarly selfless way. This selfless dedication to others is the true meaning of bodhicitta and that is why bodhicitta is not only the major prerequisite of tantra, it is also the most important fruit of this practice.

Tara

7 Dissolving Self-Created Limitations

THE BURDEN OF MISTAKEN VIEWS

So far we have seen how two of the prerequisites for pure tantric practice, renunciation and bodhicitta, help create space for us to discover our essential nature. Renunciation loosens our habitual grasping at pleasure and reliance upon externals for satisfaction, while bodhicitta opposes the self-cherishing attitude with which we focus upon our own welfare to the neglect of others. Now we will consider the third basic prerequisite: cultivation of the correct view.

In this context the correct view means the wisdom that clearly realizes the actual way in which we ourselves and all other phenomena exist. This wisdom is the direct antidote to all the mistaken conceptions we have about who we are and what the world is truly like. As long as we are burdened by these misconceptions, we remain trapped in the world of our own projections, condemned to wander forever in the circle of dissatisfaction we have created for ourselves. But if we can uproot these wrong views and banish them completely, we will experience the freedom, space and effortless happiness we presently deny ourselves.

Realizing the correct view of reality is not something mysterious. It is not a matter of staring up into space and praying for a glimpse of the truth. It is not that the wrong view is down here on the ground while the right view is somewhere up in the sky. Nor should we think that the wrong view dwells in the polluted cities of the West while the right view is to be found in the pure air of the Himalayas. It is nothing like that. The right view is available anywhere and everywhere, at all times. The beautiful face of reality exists within *all* phenomena, right here and how. It is only a matter of removing the layers of our own projections obscuring the pure vision of reality. The fault is ours, and the solution is ours.

Whenever we fix upon the idea that we exist in a certain specific way, we are hallucinating. Every time we look at ourselves in a mirror we have such a fixed idea — 'How do *I* look today? I don't want people to see *me* looking like that!' — although, in reality, we are changing all the time. We are different from one moment to the next, but still we feel we have some sort of permanent, unchanging nature.

Our view of the external world is just as deluded. Our sense organs habitually perceive things dualistically; that is, every sensory object that appears to us seems to exist from its own side as something concrete and self-contained. We think that merely because we can see, hear, smell, taste and touch these objects they must be real and true, existing solidly out there in their own right, just as we perceive them. But this concrete conception we have about how they exist is also an hallucination and has nothing whatsoever to do with their reality.

It takes time, training and clear-minded investigation to cut through these deeply ingrained wrong views and discover the actual way in which things exist. But we can begin this process right now merely by being a bit sceptical about what appears to our mind. For example, as soon as we realize that we are holding onto a solid view of ourselves — 'I am like this,' 'I should be like that' — we should remember that this view is nothing but a fantasy, a momentary projection of our mind. Nor should we passively accept that external phenomena exist in the concrete self-contained way they appear to us. It is better to be slightly suspicious of what our senses and ordinary conceptions tell us, like the wise shopper who, when buying a used car, does not immediately believe everything the salesman claims about it.

DREAMS AND EMPTINESS

If we want to understand how we are ordinarily misled by our false projections and how we can begin to break free from their influence, it is helpful to think of the analogy of our dream experiences. When we wake up in the morning, where are all the people we were just dreaming about? Where did they come from? And where did they go? Are they real or not? Of course not. These dream people and their dream experiences all arose from our sleeping, dreaming mind; they were mere appearances to that mind. They were real only as long as we remained in the dream state; to the waking mind of the next morning they are only an insubstantial memory. While we were asleep they seemed so true, as if they were really out there, having a concrete existence quite apart from ourselves. But when we wake up we realize that they were only the projections of our dreaming mind. Despite how real they seemed, these people in fact lack even an atom of self-existence. Completely empty of any objective existence whatsoever, they were only the hallucination of our dream experience.

In a very similar way, everything we experience while we are awake, including our strong sense of self, is also empty of true existence. Despite their concrete appearance of existing out there somehow, these phenomena do not in fact exist from their own side at all. Only as long as our ordinary, conventional mind is functioning, or switched on, do these relative phenomena exist for us. If this ordinary mind were to be switched off, these ordinary phenomena would cease to appear to our mind.

The point is that the people and things that make up our sensory world do not exist in the solid, objective way that they now appear to us. These appearances are nothing but the manifestations of our ordinary consciousness; they are merely apprehended or labelled by our superstitious mind. However, our basic problem is not that things *appear* to be self-existent, but that we *accept* the appearance as if it were true.

Our habit of believing in, or holding onto, merely conventional appearances as if they were most true and ultimately real has been with us since beginningless time; it is not a newly-learned philosophical view. For this reason it is not easy to overcome. However, we can begin uprooting this mistaken habit merely by realizing that the ordinary way in which we view our reality is deluded, that our instinctive belief in the self-existence of things is an invalid concept having nothing whatsoever to do with the actual way in which things exist. Understanding even this much will begin to free us from our superstitious habits. Then we can begin to wake up.

EGO-GRASPING AND INSECURITY

Not only are the things outside ourselves empty of the solid, objective reality we project onto them, the same is true for our inner sense of self. We instinctively feel that we exist as something very real, definite and substantial. We have no doubt about this real me and it seems absurd to think of it as just another hallucination. Yet if we take the trouble to search for this supposedly concrete 'I' or 'me' we will discover that we cannot find it anywhere. Neither our head, our arm, our leg nor any other part of our body is our I. The same is true of our mind: none of the countless thoughts or feelings that continuously arise and disappear is the real me. And, of course, this solid sense of self is not to be found somewhere outside this body-mind combination. Yet despite the fact that we cannot discover an independent, self-existent I anywhere, either within or outside our body and mind, we still hold onto it tightly in the very depths of our heart as if it were most real. This innate belief in something that is not true, this fundamental source of all our problems, can be called 'ego-grasping.' We did not have to learn this mistaken belief; it has been with us intuitively since birth. In fact, it was ego-grasping itself that propelled us to take birth as we did in the first place.

In what way does ego-grasping hold onto its wrong view? We can get a general idea by looking at our thoughts from moment to moment: 'How is my mind interpreting reality? Who does it believe that I am?' If our investigation is sharp enough, we will discover that we carry around with us a certain preconceived, concrete notion about ourselves — 'This is exactly who I am' — and that this notion has nothing whatsoever to do with reality.

Our ordinary ego-conception thinks, 'I definitely exist somewhere, I am real.' Not for a moment do we consider that what or who we are is only the result of giving a name or a label to a group of ever-changing mental and physical parts. Our ego-grasping mind, so intent on establishing and maintaining a solid and secure sense of identity, would never accept that the I or self is just an imputation, a mere name or designation. It asserts instead, 'I exist from my own side, inherently. I am not something merely conjured up by superstition.' But this assertion is completely mistaken. It is the wrong view that lies at the root of all our difficulties.

We are so familiar with the apparently concrete appearance of things, including ourselves, that it is not easy to switch suddenly and adopt a looser, more relaxed vision. Our ego — in this context, the neurotic mind that grasps onto a solid sense of self-identity for support — is extremely powerful and will fight against any view that threatens its security. It is deeply disturbed by the suggestion that the I, like everything else, is something merely designated by conceptual thought. Therefore we should expect a lot of resistance when we meditate on the non-self-existence of the I. This is natural; it is only our deeply ingrained ego struggling against annihilation.

IDENTIFYING THE INNER ENEMY

As long as our ego-grasping continues to project its solid, restrictive vision of reality, there will be no space in our mind to experience the expansive vision of totality that we all inwardly desire. Therefore, in order to reach beyond our false concepts and projections, first it is necessary to eliminate all the wrong ideas we have about ourselves. We need to gain as clear a picture as possible of the way we presently conceptualize ourselves, how we hold onto the false sense of ego, because there is no way of generating a correct view until we understand clearly what our habitual wrong view is like.

The great meditation masters of the past have stressed the importance of identifying as exactly as possible the conceptual nonsense of our mind. There is no benefit in using powerful techniques of insight meditation to overcome a vague or merely theoretical wrong view of self. This will not help us at all. We have to identify the root of our difficulties by looking deeply into our own mind for its characteristic misconceptions. Only then will it be possible for us to attack the fundamental cause of our problems. Otherwise it is as if our enemy were approaching from the east and we were pointing our weapons towards the west.

This point is worth emphasizing: one of the main reasons why we continue to experience the various miseries of cyclic existence, repeatedly moving from one unsatisfactory situation to another, is our inability to recognize where our problems are coming from. Even when we overcome the common mistake of thinking that our difficulties are caused externally, we still often fail to identify the inner enemy correctly. We may mistakenly conclude, for example, that the source of our dissatisfaction and frustration is a particular intellectual view or opinion that we hold and that all we have to do to correct the situation is adopt a higher, more respectable philosophical position. But such a superficial approach never strikes at the root of our difficulties.

Our basic problem is *not* an intellectual one. We may start out by subscribing to a particular analysis of who and what we are and then later change our mind and adopt an opposing view. While such a change may be intellectually satisfying, it does not solve our basic, organic problem of ego. In fact, although we may take pride in our new level of intellectual understanding, all we have done is substitute one set of supersitions for another. Instead of weakening our ego-grasping, we have merely given it something else to hold onto.

LOOSENING THE GRIP OF MISCONCEPTION

We must understand that we cannot banish our habitual concrete view of ego immediately. It takes time for this solid appearance to be overcome completely. But we can attack the grosser levels of misconception now by loosening our tight grip on what we think reality is. Then, even though the concrete appearance of things still remains, we are not so readily led astray by it.

The traditional buddhist texts illustrate this point with the analogy of a magician and his audience. By reciting hypnotic spells over pieces of wood or stone, a skilled magician can trick people into seeing horses, for example. The people affected by these spells not only see these illusory animals, they believe them to be real. They are entranced by the magician's powers and taken in by his illusions. Owing to the power of the spells, the magician also sees the horses but of course does not believe in them; he knows they are illusory because he himself conjured them up. Thus while the audience can be dazzled by the performance, the magician himself remains unmoved and unaffected.

Ordinarily, we are like the audience. We believe everything that our dualistic conceptions conjure up. If something seems to be attractive, we are immediately taken in by this superficial appearance and run after it. If its appearance changes to something not so attractive, we immediately want to run away from it, not stopping to consider how these changing appearances are a reflection of our own mind and have little or nothing to do with the object itself. As a result we are continuously led from one unsatisfactory state of existence to another, vainly seeking support for an illusory ego-identity by running after, or away from, illusory objects. In this way our life becomes an absurd drama filled with emotional conflict, frustration and disappointment.

But it is possible for us to let go of these ignorant beliefs. Like the magician, even when concrete appearances of this and that arise, we need not be swayed by them. Eventually, when our mind has become completely cleansed of all distorted views, even these dualistic appearances will cease. But we do not need to wait until then to be liberated from our conflicting emotions. The moment we start loosening our concrete conceptions we will experience a taste of this freedom.

CULTIVATING THE MIDDLE WAY

With all this talk of non-self-existence and the illusory nature of phenomena we might conclude that ourselves, others, the world and enlightenment are totally non-existent. Such a conclusion is nihilistic and too extreme. Phenomena *do* exist. It is their apparently concrete and independent *manner* of existence that is mistaken and must be rejected.

Take the example of a rainbow. Does it exist or not? Of course it does, but how? As something arising from the interplay of droplets of water in the sky, sunlight and our own point of observation. A rainbow, then, is an *interdependent* phenomenon and if we investigate we can discover its various causes and conditions. But when we gaze at this rainbow we may be so moved by its beauty that we try to reach out and touch it. Yet as we advance, the rainbow appears to retreat. No matter how fast or how far we run, we can never catch up with anything solid to grasp onto. A rainbow is by nature intangible and we have to be content with the realization that this beautiful phenomenon is an appearance that we can neither hold nor possess.

In a similar way, all existent phenomena are mere appearances to the mind; lacking concrete self-existence they come into being from the interplay of various causes and conditions. They arise, abide and disappear, all the while constantly changing. This is true of ourselves as well. No matter what our innate sense of ego-grasping may believe, there is no solid, inherent I to be found anywhere inside or outside our everchanging mental and physical components. We and all other phenomena without exception are empty of even the smallest atom of self-existence, and it is this *emptiness* (*shunyata*) that is the ultimate nature of everything that exists.

The discourses in which Shakyamuni Buddha set forth his most profound teachings on emptiness are the *Perfection of Wisdom Sutras* (a text of which is symbolically held in the left hand of Manjushri, the embodiment of fully awakened wisdom). And the Indian commentator who clarified and spread these teachings was Nagarjuna who, in addition to being a profound philosopher, was a great tantric adept, a *mahasiddha*, as well.

Nagarjuna's system of philosophical analysis is known as the Middle Way, or *Madhyamika*, for it avoids the extreme views of self-existence and non-existence, of eternalism and nihilism, of overestimation and underestimation. According to Nagarjuna, all the ordinary concepts we have of this and that are mistaken. Why? Because we habitually superimpose onto the objects of our experience qualities of concreteness, independence and self-existence, which they in fact lack. In other words, our ordinary, ignorant view of reality — both our inward sense of self and the external appearance of other phenomena such as sights, sounds and so forth — is superstitious and dualistic.

As we have discussed before, we continually project a

false image onto whatever we are dealing with and then believe that the false image is the object itself. When we gain some idea of how habitually false our dualistic vision of reality is, we may over-react and deny the existence of everything. This is the nihilistic extreme and is not only completely mistaken but dangerous as well. What we have to understand is that things *do* exist, but not in the concrete way we habitually suppose. The challenge in cultivating the correct view of emptiness is to refute completely all notions of independent self-existence without denying valid inter-dependent existence.

When we try to apply logical reasoning to prove to our-selves that something is empty — that it lacks inherent, concrete self-existence — it may sometimes feel that we are pushing too hard. 'This is empty for this reason...or that reason...or that reason.' Somehow it feels uncomfortable. This can definitely happen; strenuous application of logic can often harm our understanding rather than help it. At such times it is a good idea to relax the force of our logical investigation and merely observe how the thing we are examining functions, how it works, where it came from, and so forth. For instance, if we are examining something to discover if it is as self-existent as it appears, we can remember: 'This item was put together by people in a factory; then it was shipped to the market to be sold; then I came along and bought it; and now I am using it.' Looked at in this way, the non-self-existent nature of the thing becomes a bit clearer. We see it as something that grew out of causes, that depends on many things for its existence, that functions this way and that; this understanding will soften the general impression we have that it is something independent and concrete, existing out there as a solid, self-contained object. This approach to understanding interdependence and non-self-existence, or emptiness, is comfortable and direct. Once we are familiar with it we will easily see why many great masters of the past have claimed that interdependence, or dependent arising, is the king of logical reasoning and the best way of understanding the actual condition of things.

From Nagarjuna's point of view, there are no exceptions to the assertion that all things lack true, independent self-existence. The mind is not an exception; Buddha is not an exception. We cannot say that some unworthy object, like a garbage bin, is empty and non-self-existent, while a highly respected object, such as Shakyamuni Buddha himself, is absolute and truly self-existent. This is not so. From the point of view of their being empty and non-dualistic, the ultimate reality of Buddha and the ultimate reality of the garbage bin are identical.

The practical conclusion of all this is to refrain from immediately accepting all our dualistic appearances — this and that, good and bad, etc. — as being ultimately true, and also to refrain from denying them completely. Instead, we should remain a bit loose, a bit sceptical. We should be aware that because objects now appear to us so concretely as this and that, they have the power to lead us into conflict and confusion. If we are clearly aware of this, we will not allow ourselves to fall so readily under their spell. And if we then train ourselves to contemplate the basic clarity of the mind in which these appearances arise, we will be able to enter an experience of non-duality in which all conflict and confusion ultimately subside.

8   Clear Spaciousness of Mind

MAKING SPACE THROUGH 'NOT SEEING'

As we have discussed, renunciation, bodhicitta and the correct view of emptiness are three of the prerequisites for the practice of tantra. This does not mean, however, that our realization of these three has to be complete and perfect before we can start following the tantric path. An approximate understanding is sufficient for us to begin.

Take the realization of emptiness, for example. To gain a perfect understanding of the ultimate nature of all phenomena is a profound accomplishment. If we were to wait until then before we could practise tantra, when would we ever begin? Perhaps never! Fortunately, this is not a problem. In order to train in the various transformations of tantra, it is enough for us to be able to relax our ordinary sense of ego-identification somewhat. We do not need a perfect realization of our lack of self-existence, but we do need to be able to give ourselves some space from our ordinary, compulsive role-playing.

Tibetan lamas often say: 'Not seeing is the perfect seeing.' Strange words, perhaps, but they have a profound meaning. They describe the advanced meditator's experience of spacious, universal reality, the experience beyond dualism.

In our ordinary experience we are overwhelmed by countless dualistic perceptions and conceptions. Every day we are attracted to pleasurable objects and repulsed by unpleasant ones. Burdened with a narrow idea of who we are, we spend our time running towards this and away from that. As we have already seen, this deeply ingrained habit of viewing things dualistically and believing in our dualistic discrimi-nations leads to nothing but confusion and repeated dis-satisfaction. But it is possible to cultivate a completely different view of reality. Fed up with the endless rat-race of our compulsive cyclic existence, we can train in penetrative awareness and cultivate a direct perception of the actual way things exist.

This training proceeds in different stages, some of them highly analytical and conceptual and others more direct and experiential. Eventually, as we become more and more deeply absorbed in the experience of spaciousness, the ordinary, concrete appearances normally crowding our vi-sion begin to dissolve. Like summer clouds disappearing back into the clear blue expanse of the sky, our dualistic visions cease and we are left with nothing but the clear, empty space of non-duality. In this space empty of all concrete discriminations of this and that, our mind feels calm and boundless, free of limitation. No longer occupied with 'seeing' and believing in the ultimate reality of ordinary appearances, we enter into the 'perfect seeing' of the non-duality experience.

Far from being in a state of sleep-like blank-mindedness, our mind at such a time is awake and alert − rejecting nothing, asserting nothing, yet accepting everything. In-stead of feeling trapped and limited, forced to play the same pointless ego games over and over again, we begin to taste the true liberation of unencumbered consciousness. This liberation is possible because the superficial, conventional, fantasy, dualistic mind is *not* the fundamental nature of human beings. Our fundamental nature is as clean clear as crystal, and there is no place for the self-pitying imagina-tion. It automatically dissolves. And with it dissolve all our imprisoning limitations.

If we can enter and then remain within the naturally clear state of our own mind, we will have the time and space to see things without confusion. We will even be able to handle the business of everyday life more skilfully. Many people wonder about this. 'If I allow my mind to return to its natural, uncomplicated state, how will I be able to function in this complicated world? How can I get from one place to another? How can I hold down a job? How can I cook a meal? How can I do anything?' But there is no reason to carry on this type of argument with yourself. The fact is that when you are in a clean clear state of mind you will be free to pay full attention to what you are doing and you will therefore naturally do it well. Problems come when you are *not* living in a natural state of mind. Then, no matter what you are doing your mind will be on something else. You are supposed to be cleaning your house but your mind is thinking about going to the beach and eating ice cream. That is when you run into difficulties.

CLARITY AND NON-DUALITY

By contemplating our stream of consciousness in meditation we can be led naturally to this spacious experience of non-duality. As we observe our thoughts carefully we will notice that they arise, abide and disappear themselves. There is no need to expel thoughts from our mind forcefully; just as each thought arises from the clear nature of our mind, so too does it naturally dissolve back into this clear nature. When thoughts eventually dissolve in this way, we should keep our mind concentrated on the resulting clarity as undistract-edly as we can.

We should train ourselves not to become engrossed in any of the thoughts continuously arising in our mind. Our consciousness is like a vast ocean with plenty of space for thoughts and emotions to swim about in, and we should not allow our attention to be distracted by any of them. It does not matter if a certain 'fish' is particularly beautiful or repulsive: without being distracted one way or the other we should remain focused on our mind's basic clarity. Even if a magnificent vision arises — the kind we have been waiting years to see — we should not engage it in conversation. We should, of course, remain aware of what is going on; the point is not to become so dull-minded that we do not notice anything. However, while remaining aware of thoughts as they arise, we should not become entranced by any of them. Instead, we should remain mindful of the underlying clarity out of which these thoughts arose.

Why is it so important to contemplate the clarity of our consciousness in this way? Because, as we have seen again and again, the source of all our happiness and suffering, the root of both the pains of samsara and the bliss of nirvana, is the mind. And within the mind it is our habitual wrong view — our ignorant, insecure ego-grasping — that holds onto the hallucination of concrete self-existence as if it were reality. The way to break the spell of this hallucination is to see the illusory nature of things and recognize that all phenomena are nothing but fleeting appearances arising in the clear space of our mind. Thus the more we contemplate the clarity of our own consciousness, the less we hold onto any appearance as being concrete and real — and the less we suffer.

By watching our thoughts come and go in this way, we move ever closer to the correct view of emptiness. Seemingly concrete appearances will arise, remain for a while and then disappear back into the clear nature of our mind. As each thought disappears in this way, we should train ourselves to feel that this disappearance is even more real than the thought's original concrete appearance. The more we train in this type of 'not seeing,' the more familiar we become with the clear spaciousness of our mind. Then, even when extremely destructive thoughts and emotions such as anger and jealousy arise, we will remain in contact with the underlying purity of our consciousness. This purity is always with us and whatever delusions we may experience are only superficial obscurations that will eventually pass, leaving us with the essentially clear nature of our mind.

When you contemplate your own consciousness with intense awareness, leaving aside all thoughts of good and bad, you are automatically led to the experience of non-duality. How is this possible? Think of it like this: the clean clear blue sky is like consciousness, while the smoke and pollution pumped into the sky are like the unnatural, artificial concepts manufactured by ego-grasping ignorance. Now, even though we say the pollutants are contaminating the atmosphere, the sky itself never really becomes contaminated by the pollution. The sky and the pollution each retain their own characteristic nature. In other words, on a fundamental level the sky remains unaffected no matter how much toxic energy enters it. The proof of this is that when conditions change the sky can become clear once again. In the same way, no matter how many problems may be created by artificial ego concepts, they never affect the clean clear nature of our consciousness itself. From the relative point of view, our consciousness remains pure because its clear nature never becomes mixed with the nature of confusion.

From an ultimate point of view as well, our consciousness always remains clear and pure. The non-dual characteristic of the mind is never damaged by the dualistic concepts that arise in it. In this respect consciousness is pure, always was pure and will always remain pure.

Is the nature of deluded minds such as jealousy and anger also clear? you may ask. Yes, *all* minds equally possess this clear, immaterial nature. Whether they are positive or negative, unmistaken or deluded, all minds clearly reflect their own appropriate objects. Just as a mirror has to be clear and uncovered for it to reflect the image of the face before it, whether the face is handsome or ugly, so too must the mind be clear. If any state of mind were *not* clear, it would not reflect anything, good or bad.

We can compare positive states of mind to water at rest and deluded states of mind to turbulent, boiling water. If we investigate the nature of the boiling water we will discover that, despite the turbulence, each individual droplet is still clear. The same is true of the mind: whether it is calm or boiled into turbulence by the overwhelming complexity of dualistic views, its basic nature remains clear and conscious.

The conclusion, then, is that we all have the capacity to move from the confused, polluted state of ego-conflict to the natural clean clear state of pure consciousness itself. We should never think that our mind has somehow become irreversibly contaminated. This is impossible. If we can train ourselves to identify and enter into the natural, unaffected state of our consciousness, we will eventually experience the freedom of non-dual awareness.

MANIFESTATIONS OF CONSCIOUSNESS

From the buddhist point of view, all the circumstances of our life are manifestations of our own consciousness. This is the central understanding of Buddhism. Painful and confusing situations derive from a painful and confused mind, and whatever happiness we experience — from ordinary pleasure to the highest realization of enlightenment — is also rooted in our own mind.

If we look at our life we can easily see how it is completely controlled by our mind, especially by our mind of desirous attachment. We are continually thinking of going here and there, having this and that, and then acting on these desires, in our pursuit of satisfaction.

Not only does our restless mind continuously give birth to new thoughts and ideas, but we tend to follow them wherever they lead us. As a result we are lured from one situation to another by the promise of happiness, yet in the end we experience nothing but fatigue and disappointment. The solution is not to suppress our thoughts and desires, for this would be impossible; it would be like trying to keep a pot of water from boiling by pressing down tightly on the lid. The only sensible approach is to train ourselves to observe our thoughts without following them. This deprives them of their compulsive energy and is therefore like removing the pot of boiling water from the fire. Eventually calmness and clarity will prevail.

We humans are very proud of our ability to think, yet much of our thinking often makes things incredibly complicated. Look at the way even the wrapping of a simple piece of chocolate is crammed full of information and advertizing. We may feel that this ability to generate a great number of thoughts and ideas about a single object is a sign of our intelligence, but much of what we do with this intelligence is unnatural and totally unnecessary.

Of course our rational mind — the gross mind that is caught up in society's values — believes in the importance of everything we do. But we should not be fooled into believing that all this complicated thinking is the truth. There may be a lot of things we have to go along with in order to live our daily lives, but we don't have to believe in them. And when we are being complicated we shouldn't even believe in ourselves!

Does this mean that everything we do and think is false? No, there is some truth in what is going on. For example, even though the sky is fundamentally clear and pure, there is some truth to the pollution floating around in it. What I am saying is that we shouldn't believe that our thoughts about this and that are *absolutely* true. Air pollution may have some truth to it but it is not concrete, self-existent or ultimately real. Similarly, our thoughts may have a certain amount of truth to them, but it would be a mistake to believe in them ultimately.

What we need to learn, then, is how to maintain clear awareness while cutting off our habitual reaction to things. Ordinarily, our immediate response when something happens — when, for instance, someone gives a piece of chocolate to our friend — is to react dualistically. 'Why did she give it to *him*? Why didn't she give it to *me*? He is so lucky;

I'm so unlucky.' Our mind constantly churns out all kinds of dualistic garbage like this and our life reflects the confusion. One result is that our relationships with people and things are fickle and unstable. First we are interested in a new friend; the next day we discard him. One day we desire to own some beautiful new thing; the next day we cannot even stand to look at it. This constant changing of our likes and dislikes is another sign that our ordinary concrete concepts of reality are mistaken and nothing but the projections of a confused and superstitious mind.

There are times both in and out of meditation, however, when this dualistic confusion subsides and we experience the calm clarity of pure awareness. The peace of mind we experience at such times is indescribable and far superior to the fleeting pleasures our senses normally hunger after. But it is not enough to have an experience of this inner peace merely once or twice; this will not lead to any lasting realizations. Instead, we need continuous training so that we can repeatedly cut through our confused dualistic concepts and abide undistractedly in the underlying clarity of our essential mind. If we rely on a valid, well-tested method, such as the practice of tantra, eventually our awareness of the mind's fundamental clarity will become indestructible and we will no longer be under the control of our dualistic superstitions.

CLARITY, LOVE AND PEACE

The deep, peaceful clarity of our essential mind is in the nature of love, and in this calm atmosphere the disturbances of hatred and anger have no place. While absorbed in this deep state of awareness, there is no chance for a harmful thought to agitate us. It is not a question of consciously deciding to refrain from anger and behave virtuously; this loving, benevolent feeling arises spontaneously and effortlessly, from the depths of our being.

As this feeling of spaciousness grows and as we become closer to the correct view of non-concrete, non-self-existence, a sense of unity between ourselves and everything else will arise. Instead of feeling suffocated and oppressed by our surroundings — it's me against them — we will feel as if there is room enough for everything in the world. There *is* space for everything. Within the clear space of non-duality, everything flows freely in a constant process of coming and going, growing and dying, arising and disappearing. Within this expanse of non-self-existent reality, all things function perfectly without obstructing one another. There is no conflict, no confusion and no separation. Instead of feeling alienated from our environment, from others or even from ourselves, we share in the experience of universal harmony.

Realizing that our fundamental human quality is clear and pure allows us to cut through all partial, limiting and self-imprisoning concepts. In the clear space of the fully relaxed mind there is no distinction between *your* fundamental reality and *my* fundamental reality. One is not better than the other; one is not worse than the other. Ultimately, there is no good and bad, no pure and impure. The whole point of meditation or prayer or whatever we are trying to do is to discover the fundamental principle of human nature, to go into this deep nature, to touch our mind, the fundamental principle of totality, non-duality. The moment we reach this experience there is no room for heavy concepts, heavy emotions or sentimentality. Just be! At the moment of this experience, there are no concepts labelled by the dualistic mind. At such a time there is no Buddha, no God, no heaven or hell. Just being. The great peace. The great satisfaction.

CLARITY, COLOUR AND BLISS

Tantra contains powerful methods for awakening the very subtlest level of mind and for directing this blissful, subtle, clear-light consciousness towards the spacious and penetrating vision of non-duality. Yet even before we become highly skilled practitioners of tantra we can make contact with our mind's natural state of clarity and taste the freedom of the non-duality experience. An easy technique to use in times of confusion is simply to look up into the blue sky. Without focusing on any object, merely gaze out into space with intensive awareness and let go of all ideas about yourself. You are there, the blue infinity of space is there, and nothing else appears. As we fill our consciousness with this experience of the clarity of space, we will naturally come to contemplate the clarity of our mind.

As human beings, as soon as we visualize expansive blue light in this way our concrete conceptualizations begin to break down somehow. That is one reason why in tantric art blue is often used to symbolize non-duality, the state wherein the ordinary dualistic concepts of this and that no longer appear and are no longer held onto as real. Many people feel this freedom from conceptuality when gazing out at the vast expanse of the blue sky or the blue ocean. I am not talking about some complex philosophical notion or about something you have to accept on faith because a lama has told you it is true; I am merely relating an actual experience that many people have had and that you may have had as well.

From the tantric point of view, whenever we open our mind and senses to the objective world, our perception is always related to a particular colour. And each colour that we perceive — blue, red, green or whatever — is directly related to what is happening in our internal world. That is why in the practice of tantra, with its visualization of deities and so forth, colour and light play such an important part.

To give an idea of what I mean, let us consider the colour blue again. As I said, the particular inner quality of radiant blue light is freedom from fantasy projections. If these projections are very strong — when, for example, we are so caught up in ourselves that we cannot break out of depression — then even on a perfectly clear day we are unable to see the blueness of the sky. All we see is greyness. This definitely happens and, along with the experience of seeing red when angry or being green with jealousy, shows the close relationship between colour and states of mind.

To return to what we were discussing, we can achieve temporary freedom from conceptuality by gazing at the rays of the early morning sun or at a calm lake. We merely watch without any discrimination of this and that and at a certain point our mind will experience nothing but its own clarity. Taking such opportunities to experience clarity outwardly and then integrate it inwardly with our consciousness is a powerful and direct way of cutting through the confusion crowding our mind and of experiencing peace.

In addition to peace, whenever we contemplate the clarity of our consciousness we automatically experience a feeling of bliss as well. Normally, our dualistic mind with its confusing chatter and constant judgements about this and that tires us out. Thus it is a welcome relief when these conflicting thoughts and emotions subside and eventually disappear. The resulting clarity is experienced as peaceful, joyful and extremely pleasurable. Unlike ordinary sensory pleasures, however, the bliss that comes from such an experience brings real satisfaction. Instead of agitating our mind the way sensory pleasures ordinarily do, this bliss actually increases the strength and sharpness of our concentration.

BLISSFUL ABSORPTION INTO REALITY

Anyone who has ever tried to meditate knows that one of the biggest hindrances to concentration is the wandering thoughts that keep diverting our attention. We try to focus on a particular object only to discover that our mind has drifted somewhere else. Our attention span is almost as short as a young child's and we have great difficulty penetrating deeply into any one thing. As a result we find it impossible to gain true realizations. What is the cause of all this mental wandering? It is our overwhelming sense of dissatisfaction. We are continuously searching for something that will satisfy an undefined, inner longing, but this search is never successful. Even when we do find something pleasurable, the satisfaction it gives us is short-lived and soon we are on the look-out for something new. This restlessness is a characteristic of our dualistic mind and becomes all the more obvious when we sit down and try to concentrate in meditation.

The bliss that arises while contemplating the clarity of our consciousness is a powerful antidote to this restlessness. It has the ability to provide a calm and deep satisfaction unmatched by ordinary pleasures. Because you feel fulfilled experiencing this bliss, your mind is not even tempted to wander elsewhere, and your concentration increases effortlessly.

We have all had the experience of being so absorbed in something that we remain oblivious to things that would ordinarily distract or disturb us. Similarly, if we contemplate deeply and continuously enough upon the formless clarity of our own mind, it is possible to stop perceiving the forms, sounds, smells and so forth that come to us through the doors of our senses. As these sensory experiences and our gross conceptual thoughts subside, the gateway to superstition closes and we become aware of an upsurge of ecstatic, blissful energy from within. This tremendous surge of bliss happens spontaneously; we do not have to fabricate it in any way. And the more we experience this deep internal state of bliss, the more profound our absorption into it will become. This opens the way for us to experience expansive, liberated and all-encompassing states of consciousness that are presently unknown to us.

RIPENING OUR ENLIGHTENED POTENTIAL

The clear, pure and blissful state of mind that we have been describing exists within each one of us right now. Yet the fact that we have this fundamentally pure nature does not mean that we are already enlightened. Until we rid ourselves of hatred, greed, jealousy and all the other symptoms of the false ego shrouding our mind, we are certainly not enlightened. There is no such thing as a buddha with delusions. But beneath the gross levels at which these delusions function there is something more subtle, more basic to our nature. And it is this essential aspect of our human consciousness that has the potential of becoming fully awakened and everlastingly blissful.

The question, then, is: How can we get in touch with and fulfil the enlightened potential of our essential nature?' The practices of tantra are specifically designed to accomplish this extraordinary transformation as quickly as possible but, as we have already mentioned, we cannot jump into these practices unprepared. In other words, we need to ripen ourselves by means of the various preliminaries. The three principal aspects of the path that we have discussed — renunciation, bodhicitta and emptiness — are the common preliminaries to tantra. In addition, it is important to train in what are sometimes called the uncommon preliminaries. These include such things as receiving the appropriate tantric initiation, or empowerment, and keeping the various commitments of the empowerment, purifying oneself of obstacles to successful practice, accumulating a store of positive energy and, as will be discussed in the next chapter, gaining inspiration through the profound practice of *guru-yoga*.

Vajradhara

9 *Inspiration and the Guru*

Before we can board the lightning vehicle of tantra, we have to understand why it is both necessary and possible to abandon our ordinary, limited view of ourselves and generate in its place the enlightened self-identity of a fully evolved being. We have to realize that our low opinion of ourselves, which keeps us trapped in the cycle of perpetual dissatisfaction, only arises because we are ignorant of our basic, essentially pure nature. By generating the prerequisite renunciation, bodhicitta and wisdom, and by delving into the clear nature of our mind, we create the space in which true self-transformation can take place.

Yet it is not enough merely to know why such self-transformation is necessary and possible; we must also generate the strength and confidence that will enable us to follow this radical approach to fulfilment. In other words, we need to be inspired. We have to know that the attainment of enlightenment — completion, buddhahood, totality, or whatever we want to call it — is not only a theoretical possibility but something that people like us can and do actually achieve. In the buddhist tantric tradition the source of this inspiration is the *guru* (*lama* in Tibetan): our teacher and spiritual guide. And the root of the tantric path is unifying oneself with this source of inspiration through the practice of guru-yoga.

At the moment we are temporarily incapable of dealing

effectively with the problems created by our egotistical mind. To help solve this problem, Shakyamuni Buddha taught methods for breaking out of our ego prison and identifying ourselves with the enlightened beings of the past, present and future. Such enlightened beings have achieved a state in which there is no separation or distinction between high and low; there is only the complete equality of the enlightened experience. The practice of guru-yoga prepares us to enter this unified experience of complete fulfilment. Through seeing ourselves as one with our spiritual guide we banish the self-pitying thought: 'The buddhas are so exalted and I am nothing in comparison.' Instead, we learn to identify our innermost mind with that of our guru, who is seen as inseparable from everyone who has already achieved complete awakening.

It is through the practice of guru-yoga that our limited wisdom grows to completeness. The guru's energy of great compassion, great love, great wisdom and great skill take seed in us so that we ourselves come to embody these limitlessly beneficial qualities. We ourselves *become* the guru and, as such, can give immeasurable and inexhaustible help to all beings. If we do not generate the qualities of a true guru within us, how can we provide ultimate benefit for anyone else? We cannot even help ourselves properly.

THE INTERNAL AND EXTERNAL GURU

The tantric texts often mention that all realizations come from the guru. This is true, but we have to understand that 'guru' has two different levels of meaning. The relative, objective guru is the teacher who, by communicating with us in different ways, shows us how to act so that we can discover our own totality. But on a deeper, more subjective level, our guru is none other than our own inner wisdom, our own fundamental clarity of mind.

Look at the different ways in which people respond to the

same spiritual teachings by the same teacher. One person may not even understand intellectually the concepts contained in the teaching. Another may be able to understand them but be unable to penetrate their inner meaning. And there are those who can reach beyond the mere words and concepts and experience total unification with the teacher's wisdom and compassion. These reactions are all due to the various individuals' having achieved different levels of intellectual and spiritual evolution. The more in touch they are with their own internal guru, the more profound their understanding of the teachings will be.

Practically speaking, there is only so much the relative, external guru can do for us; he or she cannot guarantee that we gain insight and realizations. But our *inner* guru, our own clear wisdom, can accomplish everything. The practice of guru-yoga, therefore, is primarily a method for learning how to listen to this inner guru.

Ordinarily, even though we do possess this inner voice of wisdom, we do not listen to it. We do not even hear it! We are too busy listening to the garbage conversation of our gross dualistic minds. We are so accustomed to this that even when wisdom does arise, as an intuitive insight, we often reject it. By practising guru-yoga we are able progressively to cut through our superficial ways of relating to the world and make contact with the innate wisdom at the heart of our being. When we have done this, then we can communicate deeply with the outer guru as well. But as long as we are out of touch with our inner guru, no matter how profound the teachings of the outer guru may be, we will never be able to integrate them.

But we should not interpret this to mean that the external, relative guru is unimportant. This is not true; he or she is vitally important. Although it is true that the tantric teachings of Shayamuni Buddha have been in existence for 2500 years, do they exist *for us* if we have not yet met a qualified tantric master? Are they real for us or not? Despite the extensive explanations of such realized adepts as Naropa,

Marpa and Tzongkhapa, can we say that tantra is a reality for us before someone has introduced it to us? Of course not. And the same is true for the teachings of sutra as well; the fact that Buddha taught the four noble truths a long time ago does not make them true *for us*. They only become part of our reality once we have realized them, and this depends upon having met a guru who can show us their truth clearly in a way we can understand. If we do not have the living example and inspiration of the external guru, our inner wisdom will remain weak and undeveloped.

THE SPIRITUAL GUIDE AND MODEL

For the teachings of enlightened beings to reach us and for their insights to make an impression on our mind, there should be an unbroken lineage of successive gurus and disciples carrying these living insights down to the present day. As a member of this lineage, the spiritual guide who makes the four noble truths come alive for you does so through his or her inspiration or blessings. Familiar with your character and aptitudes, such a guide can make these noble truths so clean clear for you that your mind itself *becomes* the path of realization. This is what is meant by inspiration or blessing, just this. And the practice of guru-yoga, or guru devotion, is nothing more than opening ourselves to this inspiration.

Furthermore, we need an experienced guide to show us exactly how to put the teachings we receive into practice. We will not get anywhere if we try to learn from a book, hoping to figure things out by ourselves. The information may all be there, but nearly all tantric texts are cryptic, revealing their meaning only when studied together with the explanations of a skilled practitioner, and it is not easy to know just how to go about implementing this information. We need someone to show us, to give us a practical demonstration. This person is the guru.

The need for such an experienced guide is crucial when it comes to following tantra because tantra is a very technical, *internally* technical, system of development. We have to be shown how everything fits together until we actually feel it for ourselves. Without the proper guidance we would be as confused as someone who instead of getting a Rolls Royce gets only a pile of unassembled parts and an instruction book. Unless the person were already a highly skilled mechanic, he or she would be completely lost.

The main reason that religion in both the East and the West has degenerated so much nowadays is the rarity of meeting good spiritual examples. If people never meet highly realized beings they have no way of knowing the limitless possibilities of their own human consciousness. It is not enough that there are texts recording the deeds and accomplishments of past masters. By themselves, such stories cannot inspire us very much. In fact, they may only increase our feeling of remoteness: 'Buddha and Jesus lived such a long time ago,' we may think, 'and their purity belongs to another age. It is impossible for someone like myself living in this degenerate twentieth century to attain anything resembling their level of purity.' Or we may reject these accounts of past masters completely, dismissing them as fairy tales fit only for gullible children. The only way we can lay to rest these feelings of doubt, incapability and cynicism is by coming face to face with someone who has activated his or her highest potential. Only then do we have an example of purity and spiritual evolution whom we can actually see and relate to ourselves.

Thus the outer guru is of utmost importance. We need the example of someone who, while human like ourselves, has developed beyond the bounds of what we presently think possible. When we see someone who has reached beyond selfishness, who has transcended the petty concerns of this world while still living in the world, who speaks and acts from intuitive wisdom and who is truly dedicated to the welfare of others, then we can have faith and conviction that

these attainments are possible for ourselves as well. Otherwise, if our only models are those of greed and aggression,
our vision of what we are and what we can become will be
sadly limited.

A good model is important not only for those interested in
following a spiritual path. The most urgent need in the
world today is for peace and harmony, and we all feel this
need, whether we call ourselves religious nor not. But peace
cannot be brought about through mere words, and it certainly will not come about through force. Instead, we need
the example of those who have made peace and harmony
the centre of their lives. It is only the example of such
people, living lives of strength and purity, that will convince
a disillusioned world that peace — internal and external — is
truly possible here and now.

TRANSMISSION THROUGH EMPOWERMENT

For us to progress along the tantric path to complete self-
fulfilment there must be a meeting of the inner and outer
gurus. Our own enlightened potential must be energized
and inspired by contact with someone who has already
developed this potential to the full. Each tantric *sadhana*, or
method of accomplishment, focuses on a meditational deity
who embodies a particular aspect of the fully evolved,
enlightened mind. And just as the ordinary, egocentric
mind creates its own limited environment, the fully realized
mind of the deity creates its own transformed environment
within which it functions to benefit others. This combination of deity and transformed surroundings is known as a
mandala and if we wish to actualize a particular deity within
ourselves we must first be introduced into his or her mandala by a qualified tantric master. Only then will our sub-
sequent practices of self-transformation have the possibility
of succeeding.

Each tantric deity has its own unbroken lineage of practitioners. To be authentic and reliable this lineage must have had its source in the fully enlightened experience of a true master. Furthermore, this experience must have been passed down to us through an unbroken succession of adepts, each of whom attained realizations by accomplishing the practices of this deity. The strength of tantra — which has the literal meaning of 'continuous' or 'continuity' — lies in its preservation and transmission of the enlightened experience through a continuous, unbroken lineage of practitioners. Therefore, it is necessary that we establish contact with this vital lineage of transmission if we wish to transform ourselves, and the way this contact is made is through *initiation*, or *empowerment*.

Receiving an empowerment serves to awaken a special type of energy within us. By establishing an intimate communication with the guru, it arouses our potential to travel the tantric path to completion. Initiation is a shared act of meditation; it does not mean that some exotically dressed monk from Tibet is magically going to confer incredible powers on you so that you can control snakes and scorpions! We should not think of initiation in this way. Nor should we be preoccupied with the external aspects of the ceremony — the prayers, chanting, bell-ringing and so forth. What we must understand is that initiation has great *inner* significance.

There is a marvellous story about the highly accomplished tenth century Indian yogi Tilopa and his disciple Naropa that illustrates the essential nature of a tantric empowerment. Naropa was longing to receive empowerment from Tilopa and for years requested him repeatedly. But Tilopa, whose behaviour was often outrageous and unpredictable, never satisfied these requests. Sometimes he pretended not to hear Naropa; other times he answered him with apparent nonsense. But still Naropa persisted.

One day, after twelve years during which Tilopa put his

disciple through countless frustrating and dangerous situations, the two of them were walking through an arid wilderness when Tilopa suddenly announced, 'Now the time for initiation has come. Offer me a mandala!' In this context a mandala is an offering symbolic of the entire universe, and the mandala traditionally presented to the guru as a request for empowerment is generally constructed from precious and beautifully arranged objects. But there in the desert there was nothing. The only thing that Naropa could do was urinate on the ground and shape a crude mandala from the wet sand. Tilopa accepted this unusual offering and conferred the empowerment by smashing it over his disciple's head! Naropa's mind was so magnetized by this unorthodox initiation that he immediately entered into a deep and blissful state of meditative absorption (*samadhi*). Much later, when he eventually arose from this profound samadhi, his guru had disappeared. But Naropa had received what he had waited so many years for: an actual transmission of enlightened insight.

The point of telling this story is to emphasize that an empowerment is not simply a matter of ritual. Far from it. It is a special kind of communication between guru and disciple and therefore depends as much upon the disciple's openness and level of development as it does on the guru's realizations. This intimate communication activates our inner nature in such a way that we are empowered to practise uninterruptedly and complete all the attainments along the path to self-fulfilment.

Many people, both Eastern and Western, have mistaken ideas about what happens at a tantric empowerment. They think that all they have to do is attend the initiation and the lama will do the rest. 'He is giving something special and as long as I am there I will receive it.' But this is much too passive. True empowerment only occurs when there is active participation by both the disciple and the teacher. It is an act of two consciousnesses sharing the same experience. Only when this happens can it truly be said that empowerment has taken place.

RECEIVING INITIATION

Receiving an initiation requires more than just bodily participation — coming to a particular place at a particular time to receive something that someone else will be handing out to you — but active mental participation as well. We need the skill to let go and allow the experience to come, rather than being uptight and obsessive. For, you see, the initiation, including all the meditations that make it up, is a method leading us into an experience of totality and this totality is a direct antidote to our fragmented, dissatisfied, fanatical, dualistic mind. Through the inner experience of true initiation all obstacles to the realization of this totality are eliminated — eliminated not through something that you hear about or study, but through something you actually experience.

Why then do we call it an initiation? Because it is the beginning of the experience of meditation, the beginning of activating somehow our concentration, meditation and penetration into the reality of all things. Through the power of such an initiation you use the wisdom, skill and great openness of loving kindness that you already possess. There is an awakening of what already exists.

It is very important to recognize that you already have these qualities of wisdom, skill and compassion. It is a mistake to think that any of us lack them; it is a mistake to think that through empowerment we receive qualities that are totally alien to what already exists deep within us. The buddhist teachings in general and the tantric experience in particular stress that there is a limitless resource of profound wisdom and great loving kindness within each one of us already. What is necessary is that we tap this resource and activate this potential energy for enlightenment.

For an initiation to be effective, both guru and disciple must participate in creating the proper atmosphere. The guru is responsible for conducting the empowerment in such a way that it actually touches the disciples' minds, and must have the skill and flexibility to mould the initiation to fit the disciples' aptitudes. And the disciples must know how to generate an open, spacious attitude and leave the mind in such a receptive state. If they are too attached to sensory objects, or are too caught up in self-cherishing, or hold tightly onto the self-existent appearance of things, there will be no room for realizations to enter their minds. But if they have trained sufficiently in renunciation, bodhicitta and the correct view of emptiness, it will not be difficult to unburden their preconceptions and open to the transmission of insight.

When the guru and disciple are both properly qualified, the empowerment is pervaded by great blissful wisdom. Instead of remaining a requirement that must be fulfilled *before* you can enter the tantric path, the empowerment embodies the transcendentally blissful experience of the path itself. Many times in the past, in fact, disciples have attained enlightenment during the very process of initiation.

And it is important to remember that for a serious practitioner an initiation is not something that he or she receives only once. It is customary to receive initiation into a particular tantric practice again and again, each time being better able to receive deeper and deeper levels of experience. So we should not be disappointed if at first our meditation stays only at the level of mere imagination rather than true experience. That is still good enough; don't think that it's not. Merely to imagine an experience plants seeds in the vast field of your consciousness and eventually these seeds will ripen into the actual experience itself. This is a natural progression. So you should always remain open and relaxed and be satisfied with whatever happens.

THE FORMAL PRACTICE OF GURU-YOGA

Once we have received an initiation into the practice of a particular meditational deity we may begin our daily practice of that deity's *sadhana*, and one of the first meditations of the sadhana is the practice of guru-yoga, done in a way similar to the following. Either in front of us or above the crown of our head we visualize the main meditational deity of the tantra we are practising surrounded by the various gurus of its lineage. These lineage gurus are the successive masters who have passed on the teachings and realizations of that particular practice and include everyone from the first master of the lineage through to our own spiritual guide, the guru from whom we received the empowerment.

We then request the members of this assembly to bestow their inspiration and blessings upon us and, in response to this request, they merge with one another, enter us through the crown of our head in the form of light, descend our central channel (see Chapter 10) and dissolve into our heart centre. As this happens, all ordinary dualistic appearances and conceptions dissolve into the clear space of emptiness. We then meditate upon the feeling that our guru, who in essence is identical with the deity, and our own subtle consciousness have become indistinguishably one.

The essence of the guru is wisdom: the perfectly clear and radiant state of mind in which bliss and the realization of emptiness are inseparably unified. Therefore, when we visualize the guru absorbing into our heart we should feel that an indestructible impression of that wisdom is being made upon our fundamental mind. From this time onwards we should try to recall this inner experience of great bliss and non-dual wisdom repeatedly, no matter what circumstances we may encounter. If we let our mindfulness of this inner experience deteriorate, we will easily fall under the influence of grosser sensory experiences and the inner bliss of non-dual wisdom will eventually vanish completely.

When we visualize our spiritual guide as the meditational deity we should think especially about his or her great kindness and concern for us. Simply speaking, although the guru-deity is not my father, not my mother, not my wife, not my husband, *still* he is as concerned about me and my situation as if he were. It is as if he exists solely for my sake, so that I might develop a supremely healthy body and mind. This is how we should relate to the visualized guru-deity.

By visualizing in this way and thinking of the personal kindness shown to you by your guru, a powerful connection is established. Instead of being some vague, impersonal image, the deity is seen as being inseparable in essence from your own immeasurably kind spiritual guide. In this way a feeling of incredible closeness develops. Because of this feeling of intimacy and because the deity is visualized as a radiantly beautiful being of light, inspiration can come to you very quickly. Your visualization magnetically attracts such inspiration, such blessing, and this enables you to develop clear realizations. This, after all, is the entire point of the guru-yoga practice. The purpose for seeing the guru in an exalted aspect has nothing to do with benefiting the guru — a true guru has no use of such homage — but is solely to speed your own spiritual evolution.

CONTINUOUS RECOGNITION OF UNITY

Seeing the underlying unity of our guru, the deity and ourselves is not something we do only during formal meditational practice. We need to practise guru-yoga — identifying ourselves with the guru's essential buddha nature — during every moment of our life. Instead of always thinking about our miserable, dissatisfied mind, we should cultivate the recognition of our fundamental unity with the absolute guru residing within. Even if our most egotistical mind is arising, instead of adding fuel to it by identifying strongly with this deluded state, we should try to recognize *that very mind* as the enlightened totality of the guru-buddha nature: the so-called *dharmakaya* experience (see Chapter 10). Then suddenly even this deluded mental energy can be utilized and transformed in such a way that it is digested into great wisdom. This is the outstanding teaching of tantra.

To be able to accomplish such a profound transformation,

however, we must practise guru-yoga continuously. We must become intimately familiar with the essential oneness of the guru, the deity and our own innermost nature. In *Offering to the Spiritual Master* it is said, 'You are the guru, you are the deity, you are the daka/dakini, you are the dharma protector.' To interpret this we can borrow an image from Christianity, a spiritual tradition based on the existence of one God, one absolute reality. Although God manifests in the three aspects of Father, Son and Holy Spirit, God is essentially one: the principle of totality. Similarly, although tantra speaks about many different deities, dakas, dakinis, protectors and so forth, at a certain point all these apparently different entities are to be seen as a unity, one all-embracing totality. That is the fundamental concern of tantra. When you develop yourself fully so that your entire inner potential is realized, then you yourself *become* a deity, you yourself *become* a buddha. This is the ultimate aim of guru-yoga.

TOUCHING THE HEART WITH INSPIRATION

A common problem for all of us is that our knowledge of so-called spiritual matters is often just in our head, not in our heart. We are proud of how much we have studied and learned about the world's religions and may even have mastered the vocabulary of their philosophy and meditational practices, yet still we remain basically unsubdued and deluded. We Tibetans often say: 'Although butter is used to soften leather, the leather container in which the butter is stored remains stiff and inflexible.' Despite the fact that spiritual understanding is meant to soften our concrete, limiting preconceptions and subdue our delusions, it is nevertheless possible to contain a lot of intellectual knowledge about religion while remaining unchanged by it. A dry, intellectual approach to spiritual matters leaves our heart untouched and unaffected.

What is lacking is the proper inspiration, or blessing, in

our mind. We have to be convinced by some kind of heartfelt, living experience of the existence and effectiveness of a potent spiritual reality both inside and outside ourselves. Otherwise our wisdom eye remains closed and we are incapable of perceiving this profound reality no matter how much we might have studied.

As we have discussed, it is the guru who provides this necessary inspiration, this link between our consciousness and the actual experience of transcendence. In the behaviour of our own guru we can see for ourselves the beneficial effects of training the mind in love and wisdom. By thinking of our guru's lifetime devotion to others and his or her lack of self-cherishing, as well as upon the many other excellent qualities our guru embodies, and then by dissolving and absorbing the entire lineage of gurus into our heart, we are enabling these enlightened qualities to take root deep within us. It has been the experience of generations of gurus and disciples that the repeated practice of such visualizations, done in conjunction with the letting go of our concrete conceptions of self, has a profound effect on the mind and can transform dry, intellectual knowledge into an organic experience of insight.

While engaged in the practices of guru-devotion we should be patient and proceed gradually. It is extremely important not to force ourselves, to do what does not feel right out of some misplaced sense of obligation; I am thinking particularly of the practice of seeing the guru as inseparable from the meditational deity. In truth, we cannot see their essential unity until we have developed some measure of the deity's qualities within ourselves. So we should not push. It would be a great shame if our practice of these profound tantric techniques were to degenerate into a custom we felt somehow obliged to follow, the way many church-goers attend religious services merely because it is something they think society expects them to do. To avoid this, we should allow our practices to develop at their own pace. Eventually, as we grow more and more familiar with the fundamental nature of our own mind as well as with the good qualities of the guru and the positive effects of meditating upon the deity of light, we will come to appreciate the profundity of these guru-yoga practices more and more completely.

BREAKING THE HABIT OF ORDINARY APPEARANCES

The various practices of tantra are designed to help us overcome not only our vain dependence upon ordinary pleasures but also our habitual acceptance of ordinary appearances and conceptions. From beginningless time we have been brainwashed into believing in the ultimate reality of the world shown to us by our five extremely limited and dualistic senses, and now we are trying to break this deeply ingrained habit. This is not easy to do; our baby wisdom of emptiness is easily overwhelmed by our gross sense consciousnesses. We are like the scientist who knows from investigation and reasoning that a table, for instance, is nothing more than a momentary configuration of ceaseless energy yet still has great trouble seeing it as anything but a solid, static object. That is why we have to train again and again in those visualization practices that dissolve our false notion of concrete self-existence and strengthen our understanding and experience of non-duality.

A major difficulty facing us is that we naturally have a much easier time accepting the reality of our gross sensory experiences than we do believing in the reality of our visualizations. It is common to feel, 'Although I can see myself as made of light, this is just a game that I am playing with my mind. It is not real. But my physical body *is* real; I can actually touch it and see it in a mirror.

What we have to learn is that the experiences we have through our imagination and those we have through our senses are actually the same! Both exist only for the particular mind experiencing them; they have no ultimate reality from their own side. A major difference, however, is that our ordinary sensory experiences keep us bound to the circle of continually recurring dissatisfaction and suffering while our visualizations of conscious bodies of light, and practices such as the absorption of the guru, introduce us to the very subtle, fundamental level of our being. With this very subtle mind of clear light we can break out of the prison of our ordinary gross conceptions and experience the unceasing happiness of full enlightenment.

If you have not yet tasted the bliss of your fundamental mind, and have not seen for yourself how you can achieve a state of penetrative awareness and openness far surpassing what you now feel is possible, naturally you will be very sceptical. You probably think that the pleasure you feel, say, when you eat your ice cream is real, and that whatever bliss you might experience during meditation is just an illusion. The only way of overcoming such scepticism is by becoming more and more familiar with your own inner reality until eventually it is undeniable. And it is by practising guru-yoga, and the other transformative methods that follow from it, that familiarity with the deeply blissful character of your own mind is achieved.

10 *Entering Highest Tantric Practice*

THE VAJRA BODY AND RESIDENT MIND

According to highest yoga tantra, our body and mind exist not only on the gross level we are normally familiar with but also on subtle levels about which most of us are completely unaware. Our ordinary physical form, composed of various material elements, is subject to the inevitable sufferings of sickness, decay and death: merely possessing it binds us to the recurring miseries of our ordinary existence. But within the boundaries, or atmosphere, of this body is another, far more subtle, body: the so-called *vajra body*, 'vajra' having the connotation of indestructible. Just as our gross and perishable physical body is pervaded by the ordinary nervous system, this subtle vajra body is pervaded by thousands of channels (*nadi*) through which flow the energy winds (*prana*) and drops (*bindu*) that are the source of the bliss so vital to highest tantric practice.

As is true of our essentially pure and blissful mind, this subtle conscious body exists within us right at the present moment, and the job of the tantric practitioner is to discover and make use of it. Once we have made contact with this clear, conscious body of light through meditation our gross physical body will no longer be a problem for us for we will have transcended it. Physical limitations are just another symptom of ego-grasping and once we merge with our essentially pure nature all such restrictions will be overcome. At that point, the attainment of the radiant light body of the deity (see p.124) ceases to be merely a visualized goal and becomes a reality.

This is not the place to discuss the vajra body and its channels, winds and drops in detail, but it will be helpful to mention the central channel (*avadhuti* or *shushuma*) at least briefly because it is of particular importance. This channel runs in a straight line from the crown of our head down to an area in front of the base of our spine, and along it are several focal points known as *chakras*, or energy wheels. Each one serves a different function in the practice of tantra. Depending upon which tantra we are following and which stage or function we are focusing upon in our meditation, we turn our concentrated attention towards and penetrate a particular centre. It is not a matter of guessing which centre to choose; these things are described in precise detail in the tantric texts and their commentaries and are explained to the qualified practitioner by the spiritual guide.

The most important chakra, however, is the one located at the level of the heart, for the heart chakra is the home of our very subtle mind: the priceless treasure of all tantric practitioners. This very subtle mind has been with us from conception; in fact, together with its supporting energy wind, the continuum of this mind has been with us for lifetimes without beginning. As the fundamental consciousness abiding at our heart centre throughout this life, the very subtle mind is sometimes referred to as our residential mind. However, although it has flowed continuously from life to life, it has rarely had the opportunity to function. What prevents it from becoming activated − and from performing its most valued function: penetrating the universal nature of reality – is the continual arising of our numerous gross states of mind. These are like tourists, temporary visitors who come and go in constant movement, and they completely overwhelm the stationary resident mind.

The activity of all types of mind, both gross and subtle, depends upon their supporting energy winds and upon where these winds are travelling. As long as they flow through any of the thousands of channels other than the central one, these winds activate the gross tourist minds that repeatedly give rise to superstition and confusion — our ordinary life experiences. But when these winds enter, abide and dissolve into the central channel – as happens naturally at the time of death, for example – these gross minds subside and the very subtle mind of clear light arises instead.

With the dissolution of the energy winds into the central channel, the environment in which our gross minds normally function automatically disappears, the tourist department is closed and our superstitious thoughts can no longer come and go. In the resulting quietness our original, fundamental consciousness – the resident mind – awakens.

This entire process happens automatically during the death process but very few people are trained to take advantage of the very subtle clear light consciousness that arises at that critical time. In fact, few people even recognize it. But the tantric yogi and yogini train themselves not merely to recognize this blissful consciousness at the time of death but to awaken this penetrating clear light mind during their life in meditation, thereby gaining complete control over it. By cultivating a profound concentration on the vajra body in general and upon the central channel in particular, they are able to cut through the gross levels of mental functioning and make contact with their original mind. They can use this powerfully concentrated mind to meditate on the emptiness of self-existence and penetrate the ultimate nature of reality, thereby freeing themselves of all delusions. At the same time that this total absorption into the clear space of non-duality takes place, they experience an explosion of indescribably blissful energy. The unity of great bliss and the simultaneous comprehension of emptiness (the tantric experience known as *mahamudra*, the great seal) is the quickest path to full enlightenment.

CHANGING OUR VIEW OF DEATH

The dissolution of our vajra body's energy winds into the central channel is crucial to advanced tantric practice, and because this dissolution takes place naturally when we die we should become as familiar as possible *now* with the process of death.

Many of us, however, have a great reluctance to examine, or even think about, death. We are frightened and find the whole subject extremely distasteful. But it is essential for us to know how our mind operates, not only during the day but while we sleep and at the time of death as well, and this requires educating ourselves about things that we have often avoided up until now. If we examine these matters we will find that death, instead of being a horrifying black hole that is waiting to suck us in and devour us, is a potential source of great comfort and even joy.

We generally think that dying is something negative, but this is just our projection. In fact, dying can be a lot better than the experiences we ordinarily think of as pleasurable because these ordinary experiences cannot give us tremendous bliss and peace. A beautiful flower, say, can give us something but not the extraordinary bliss and peace that the death experience can. A boyfriend or girlfriend may be able to give us a certain amount of pleasure or bliss but cannot solve any of our fundamental problems; they can give only a temporary solution to some of our more superficial emotional problems. But at the time of death *all* our emotional problems and all our anxiety end. As all the conflicting concepts of this and that naturally disappear into space, the way is open to experience extraordinary penetrative insight. What we have to realize, therefore, is that death is not a sudden and terrifying annihilation but a gradual process during which our mind grows more and more fine and subtle. If we want to practise highest tantra, or even if we merely want to prepare for what we must all eventually encounter, we should become as familiar with this gradual process as we can now. If we wait until the moment of death itself it will be too late.

DEATH, INTERMEDIATE STATE AND REBIRTH

The sutra and tantra teachings diagnose the problems of

cyclic existence in different ways, and also offer different solutions to these problems. According to sutra, the root of samsaric suffering is ego-grasping: the wrong view that holds onto a mistaken belief in a self-existent "I", or ego-identity. The antidote for this ignorant conception is found by cultivating a completely opposite view. Instead of ignorantly assenting to our instinctive belief in self-existence, we are taught how to generate an insight into emptiness: the total negation of all notions of independent self-existence. Thus in sutra much emphasis is placed on removing our wrong view and replacing it with the opposing correct view.

While the lightning path of tantra does not deny what sutra has to say, it offers a different, more radical approach to the problems of our life. According to these more advanced teachings, all difficulties are rooted in our ordinary uncontrolled experiences of death and what happens after death. By dying uncontrollably we are forced to enter an uncontrolled intermediate state (*bardo*), and from there we experience uncontrolled rebirth leading to yet another uncontrolled life and death. In this way the wheel keeps spinning, dragging us from one unsatisfactory state of existence to another.

It should be emphasized again that death is anything but a problem; it is a precious opportunity. For the person who is well prepared, the dying process offers an unequalled opportunity to experience what he or she has always been searching for: the subtle, penetrating and supremely blissful mind of clear light. However, although such a blissful mind arises automatically during the death process, most of us are unable to take any advantage of it at all. Our death, like our life, goes by without conscious, clear-minded control, and what could have been the gateway to liberation becomes instead a passage into yet another lifetime of confusion.

The cure for such uncontrollably recurring confusion is a type of meditation in which we transform our ordinary experiences of death, bardo and rebirth into the enlightened experience of a buddha. The tantric antidote, therefore, is not something that is the opposite of the problem — the way that the wisdom of emptiness is the opposite of the ignorance of ego-grasping — but rather something that is similar to it. Because the cure is similar to the disease, forces that ordinarily lead to confusion and suffering can be used to bring about clarity and self-fulfilment instead. This is one of the reasons why tantra is such a speedy and, if practised incorrectly, dangerous path.

THE THREE ASPECTS OF BUDDHAHOOD

In order to understand how tantra handles the problems of death, bardo and rebirth, we need to know something about the three so-called bodies (*kaya*) of a buddha. When all the veils currently obscuring our mind have been removed and when all of our positive potentials have been developed to their utmost, there is the simultaneous achievement of the truth body (*dharmakaya*), enjoyment body (*sambhogakaya*) and emanation body (*nirmanakaya*) of a buddha. The dharmakaya is the unlimited and unobstructed *mind* of an enlightened being while the remaining bodies are the two levels on which this mind manifests itself in order to benefit others. (It is said that the dharmakaya represents the accomplishment of one's own purpose through the attainment of unexcelled qualities of mind, while the sambhogakaya and nirmanakaya represent the accomplishment of others' purposes through a buddha's spontaneous manifestation in forms to which unenlightened beings can relate.)

The experience of these three kayas is the experience of total enlightenment. As unenlightened beings we do not have this experience yet, but we can have something similar to it. It is not only true that we *can* have it, but according to the resultant path of tantra, we *should* have it! Such an ambitious attitude accords well with an attitude prevalent in the West: 'I want the best and I want it right now!' The difference is that ordinarily we are striving mainly after material things, but when we practise tantra we are seeking to bring the blissful experience of full conscious control over every aspect of our life into our present reality.

TAKING ADVANTAGE OF OUR HUMAN FORM

Turning the experience of death, bardo and rebirth into the path to enlightenment is not a fantasy. Because we have the type of body we do, we can definitely accomplish this great aim. According to the sutra teachings, our present physical body is viewed largely as a hindrance. It is decaying from moment to moment, prone to sickness and attracts misery in the way a magnet attracts pieces of iron. In fact, the most succinct way of defining the first noble truth of suffering is to say it is the body itself. But the tantric teachings take the opposite view. Far from being a hindrance or obstacle, the human body is regarded as something most precious because it contains all the necessary equipment for reaching enlightenment in one lifetime. It is made up of the four elements of earth, water, fire and air and the energies (*prana*) associated with them. And because it is born from the womb, it contains the red and white drops — from the mother and father respectively — needed for arousing the blissful energy of the kundalini experience.

We are fortunate to have this type of body and should not waste the precious opportunity it gives us to realize our full potential. We should not be like those people who do not know how to use their natural resources properly. For example, I know of some Nepalese farmers who cut down mango trees for firewood. It takes so many years for a mango tree to grow and its fruit is so precious, but these people do not seem to appreciate this. Instead of making good use of what they have, they destroy these precious trees, lose their land through erosion and are left with nothing. If we neglect to use our body's precious energy for the attainment of enlightenment, and squander it instead on the meaningless pursuits of this life, then we are far more ignorant than those farmers. Rather, we should be like those ingenious scientists who know how to extract energy from everything — from sunlight, the tides, wind and so forth — and who also know how to put this energy to constructive use. In other words, we should be skilful, and the highest skill involves transforming our present body from a source of pain and dissatisfaction into the blissful path to unsurpassed happiness for ourselves and others. This is the ultimate goal of all tantric practice.

THE PROCESS OF DYING

When the totality of one's enlightened nature is realized, the dharmakaya, sambhogakaya and nirmanakaya are achieved simultaneously. But in terms of tantric practice, these three kayas, or bodies, gradually evolve in a sequence mirroring the natural unfolding of death, the intermediate state and rebirth. So, as was indicated earlier, first we should understand how the process of death and so forth ordinarily occurs; then we can understand how they are transformed into the three bodies of enlightenment.

Death is the separation of the mind from the body. This separation may take place over several hours or days, as is generally the case in a death from natural causes, or it may happen rather more suddenly, as in an accident. But in either case there are certain definite stages in the dying process. The body does not lose its ability to maintain consciousness all at once, but does so gradually with each element of the body — earth, water, fire and air — losing its supportive ability in turn.

The tantric texts dealing with the dying process describe the first four stages of death in vivid terms. They say that first the earth element sinks, or dissolves, into the water element and that then the water element sinks into the fire, and fire into the air, and the air element into consciousness itself. Such a description is useful for meditation but should not be taken literally. For example, when it is said that the earth element 'sinks' into the water element, this means that as the solid portions of the body are gradually losing their ability to function and are becoming less intimately interconnected with the dying person's mind, the liquid elements appear stronger and more evident.

As these various physical elements become stronger and weaker in turn, the dying person experiences certain external and internal signs associated with each stage of the dissolution process. As these signs are listed in great detail in other texts, it is not necessary to mention them all here. However, it will be helpful to point out some of the visions that typically occur.

When ordinary people die they are out of control. Because they have not trained themselves during their life, they are overwhelmed by the experience of death and bewildered as their bodily elements go out of balance and cease functioning harmoniously. It seems to them as if they were in the middle of a violent earthquake and it is therefore very difficult, if not impossible, for them to remain calmly aware of what is happening. Death is thus experienced as a series of frightening hallucinations, a nightmarish disaster. Yet for someone who is prepared the same visions that cause panic in others can bring an extraordinary peace. And for those advanced practitioners who have trained their minds well, each stage of the dissolution process brings ever increasing clarity and insight.

According to buddhist psychology, whether an object brings satisfaction or not depends upon a decision made beforehand by your consciousness. Even before you see a particular thing your mind has already decided, 'This will make me happy.' Then when you actually contact it with your eyesight you think, 'Oh, this is very nice.' The same is true for a negative reaction. If your consciousness has already decided that you do not like a certain person, then when you actually meet him you will see nothing but an unpleasant person. In other words, all the seemingly real *good* things that we like and *bad* things that we dislike are, in fact, creations of our own mind.

How is all of this related to our death experiences? Buddhism teaches that the way to experience both a happy life and a happy death is by recognizing exactly what is happening without being misled and confused by appearances. During our life we experience one dissatisfaction after another because we mistakenly believe that what appears to us as good or bad *truly* exists in this way. We therefore spend all our time and energy running after this and away from that. During our lifetime we build up such a strong habit of relating to things in this alternatingly greedy and fearful way that it is only to be expected that at the time of our death, when everything seems to be falling apart, we will be overwhelmed by great confusion.

The solution is to learn to see all things as mere appearances to the mind, as lacking even one atom of independent self-existence. We need to understand that, in this respect, all things are like illusions. The same understanding should be applied to the visions that appear one after the other as our consciousness goes through the dying process. We should become familiar with what to expect when we die so that we can deal with these illusions instead of being overwhelmed and confused by them. The key, during both life and death, is to recognize illusions as illusions, projections as projections and fantasies as fantasies. In this way we become free.

DEATH AND DHARMAKAYA

First of all let us consider what might happen to us if, totally untrained and unprepared, we were to die in a state of great anxiety and bewilderment. Desperately holding tightly onto a supposedly solid sense of 'I' for security, we panic as the basis of our ego-identity — our body itself — begins to disintegrate. As the earth element of our body deteriorates and the water element seems to grow stronger, our mind is filled with the hallucination of a shimmering silver-blue mirage. We feel trapped and suffocated, as if our body were buried in the earth or caught in an avalanche. Then the water element sinks into the fire element and a vision of swirling smoke appears. As this is happening we may feel as if we are drowning or being carried away by violent currents of water. Next, the fire element dissolves and our body gradually grows colder; we perceive a vision like that of sparks dancing over an open fire at night. During this process some dying people cry out, thinking that their body is being consumed by flames. Finally, the wind, or air, element dissolves, our breathing grows shallow, and we may feel that we are being blown about like a leaf in the wind. Along with this experience comes the vision of a dying flame in a darkened room. As is the case when a candle is about to go out, the flame suddenly grows brighter as if exploding in a final burst of energy. Our breathing, which has been getting more and more difficult, now comes to a complete halt. To the outside world we now seem to be dead (and this is often the signal for those gathered around us to burst into tears).

But we are not dead yet. The four gross elements and the conceptual minds associated with them have ceased to function but there remain subtle levels of consciousness still to be absorbed. This happens as the subtle white drop received from our father at conception and located during our life at the crown of our head and the red drop received from our mother and located at our navel come towards each other and eventually meet at the level of our heart. As the white drop descends we perceive a vision of empty space pervaded by whiteness, and as the red drop rises we perceive a similar vision of empty space, this time pervaded by redness. Finally the two drops meet, forming a sphere enclosing our very subtle, fundamental consciousness and its associated wind at our heart, and we experience the blackness of a completely darkened room. This darkness becomes blacker and blacker until we eventually fall into total unconsciousness.

But still we are not dead. Within this sphere at our heart centre resides our very subtle consciousness and its associated subtle energy wind. After some time — which can be as long as three days even for an untrained person — this sphere opens and our mind is illuminated. The very subtle mind awakens and nothing appears to it but the vision of empty space, clear and luminous. This clear light consciousness is the last and most subtle of all the states of mind experienced during this lifetime.

For an ordinary person all these absorptions — from the appearance of the mirage-like vision to the dawning of the clear light — are uncontrolled. They happen one after the other but we are barely conscious of them; our mind is too confused and distracted. But those who have trained themselves well beforehand maintain clear awareness of everything that is happening during this process. They know which vision will come next and understand that everything they are perceiving is merely an appearance to their dying mind, empty of all independent self-existence as something truly out there. Because of this understanding they are not frightened by what they see. Instead, as their mind grows more and more subtle, their awareness of the emptiness of true existence becomes more and more penetrating. Finally, with the arisal of the clear light, this very subtle mind mixes indistinguishably with emptiness in an experience of inexpressible bliss. For such a person, death has become the precious opportunity for perfecting the wisdom of non-duality. By means of this clear and unobstructed wisdom the trained practitioner has transformed the ordinary death process into the enlightened dharmakaya experience.

The dharmakaya experience of non-duality is beyond words, beyond expression, beyond concepts. When someone speaks about this experience, therefore, there is always the danger of being misinterpreted. So you should not trust my words; they are only the false words of my superstition. No matter how skilful they may be, words still come from the limited conceptual mind and are understood by the same limited mind. What is necessary is to touch the experience itself and thus go beyond the words used to describe it. That is why tantra puts such emphasis upon action rather than theory.

Although it is a good thing to study the various buddhist texts and commentaries and learn to analyze them with a sharp and critical intelligence, we should understand that there are times when this analytical approach is actually harmful. One of my meditation masters once told me, 'At a certain point you have to abandon the philosophical way of understanding things. You must go beyond debate, beyond argument.' That shocked me! I was a young, enthusiastic student at the time and liked to analyze and criticize everything I heard. But I eventually understood what he meant: remaining caught up in intellectual preconceptions can prevent us from entering profound meditational experiences. So, it is important to know when to relax, let go and allow the mind to settle into its natural state of clarity.

Truly qualified masters of all traditions always stress that there are certain times when you should not be doing analytical or intellectual activity at all. For instance, it would be a great mistake to engage in analytical thought during the advanced completion stage practices of highest yoga tantra (which we will discuss later). Why? Because when you use your intellect it is natural for all sorts of superstitious concepts to arise. Your mind becomes overly busy and vibrates with the fragmented energy of such concepts. Then, since every state of mind is associated with its own wind, or air, energy, your subtle nervous system will also become busy vibrating with various conflicting wind energies. This not only interferes with the control you are trying to gain over your nervous system through these completion stage practices, but it can also easily lead to a painful condition the Tibetans call '*lung*,' meaning frustrated energy at the heart. As with all aspects of the spiritual path, there is a time to use the intellect and there is a time to put it aside.

BARDO AND SAMBHOGAKAYA

For ordinary people, once the clear light is finished, the

mind experiences the visions of the dharmakaya experience just described but in a reverse order, from the darkness of unconsciousness to the mirage-like vision. With the beginning of this reverse process, our mind departs from our body and death actually occurs. Immediately thereafter we enter the intermediate state, the bardo, and here again our mind is completely out of control. With the speed of thought we are propelled from one situation to another, as in a dream. But this dream is more often a nightmare. Sometimes terrifying visions, arising from the imprint of our past delusions and negative actions, appear and cause us to run away in fear. At other times alluring visions arise and we run after them with intense craving, only to be disappointed. This is what happened, after all, when we were still alive and possessed an ordinary physical body; our life was spent in a constant search for security, running away from this and after that. But now our situation is even more extreme. Because our insubstantial bardo body is made of nothing but subtle energy wind, it can pass through matter without any obstruction and therefore we enter without hindrance into whatever situation our fearful, craving mind throws us.

This is the ordinary bardo experience, but once again trained practitioners can transform it into the path to enlightenment. Well versed in the practices of the rainbow-like illusory body, once the clear light of death comes to an end they assume a clear, radiant body of light instead of the deluded bardo body. In this way they transform the ordinary bardo into the enlightened sambhogakaya, or enjoyment body, experience.

REBIRTH AND NIRMANAKAYA

Just as the ordinary process of death and bardo are uncontrolled, compelled by the force of our deluded grasping, so too is our ordinary rebirth. We are eventually blown by the winds of our deluded actions *(karma)* to where our future parents lie in sexual embrace. There, with our mind experiencing a confused mixture of longing desire and repulsion, we faint and are thereafter conceived in our mother's womb. From this impure beginning a life full of impurity and suffering follows. Our body — deriving from the sperm and egg of our parents — is subject to the miseries of birth, sickness, ageing and eventually death, while our mind — as a stream flowing from our previous life — continues under the compulsion of insecure craving, repulsion and ignorance to create the causes for further dissatisfaction and suffering.

This ordinary rebirth experience can be transformed by the skilled practitioner in the same way that death and bardo were transformed. Instead of moving from the bardo to the next life under the force of insecurity and grasping, ignorantly falling into unconsciousness, the well-trained followers of tantra can choose their rebirth consciously. Having trained themselves in the practice of overcoming ordinary appearances, they can see their future parents as male and female deities and themselves as a deity as well. Depending on their level of control and the type of training they have completed, they may even take rebirth in a pure land: a state of existence in which everything is conducive to the attainment of enlightenment. Even if they are born on this earth they can choose a situation suitable to spiritual development so that they can continue to practise until the totality of enlightenment is reached. With such full awareness and complete control over their next life, ordinary rebirth can be transformed into the enlightened experience of the nirmanakaya, or emanation body.

This has been only a brief account of the way the tantric practitioners can transform ordinary death, bardo and rebirth into the three bodies of an enlightened being, but it is enough to give us a clear idea of what lies at the heart of the highest tantric practice. Up until now we have been overwhelmed by the forces of ignorance, karma and our many delusions with the result that we have been going around in a circle of birth, death and rebirth without choice or control over and over again. Until we replace our ignorance with wisdom and transform these three recurring events into the enlightened experience of a buddha, we will continue going around in this vicious circle forever, searching for happiness but finding only disappointment.

CUTTING REBIRTH

It is not difficult to understand how ordinary death, bardo and rebirth experiences are the root of our difficulties. Because we live, die and are reborn with an uncontrolled mind and body, we have to experience the many mental and physical sufferings of ordinary life. Stated simply, if we were not born in the first place there would be no way for these problems to arise! Through the practice of highest tantra, we can avoid such a birth, and all its problems, completely.

Some people might be confused when hearing that the proper practice of tantra can cut rebirth. 'What is the point of this? Why should I give up the chance to return to the world? Is this what the path is leading me to: total non-existence? If so, I am not interested!'

To avoid this confusion we should realize that 'cutting rebirth' has a very specific meaning: namely, to free ourselves from having to experience *uncontrolled* rebirth again and again. We can practise tantra successfully and still return to this world. In fact, our compassionate bodhicitta motivation makes it unthinkable that we would abandon others; it pledges us to return for their sake. Shakyamuni Buddha himself did so and his birth, far from being a problem, was the source of limitless benefit. At the moment, however, *our* rebirths take place without control and merely perpetuate the beginningless cycle of misery. This is what needs to be cut. The same is true for death and bardo; it is the *uncontrolled* experience of these events that must be eliminated and transformed.

Our uncontrolled life, in which the three poisons of attachment, anger and ignorance play such a big part, leads inevitably to an uncontrolled death, during which these same delusions give rise to even greater confusion. Our mind is overwhelmed by the hallucinations associated with the dissolution of the various bodily elements and we enter the intermediate state with tremendous fear and longing. There, because we possess a body of consciousness rather than one of gross physical form, our superstitions have an even stronger effect upon us. Each delusion that surfaces in our mind immediately throws us into a correspondingly deluded situation. This is an extremely frightening condition and eventually, when we perceive the vision of our future parents, our longing for security propels us to take rebirth — and the cycle begins again. Nowhere is there any rest or peace as the security and happiness we seek always elude us. This is the symptom of our ordinary samsaric existence.

The aim of tantric practice is to free ourselves from these recurring difficulties by helping us to break out of this vicious circle. By training our mind to overcome the tyranny of ordinary, deluded appearances and by preparing beforehand for what we must eventually encounter as one life draws to an end and another begins, we are generating the ability to substitute the enlightened experience of the three bodies of a buddha for the usual confusion of death, bardo and rebirth.

Heruka

11 *Arising as a Deity*

The most important thing about tantric practice is to get a taste, an actual experience, of something that has meaning for you. It doesn't matter how small the piece of chocolate you get is; you taste it and you are satisfied. That is all. So those people who get something really clear in their mind and then, the minute they understand it, put it directly into their heart — these are the people who are truly practising. They are the ones who are getting the chocolate.

Our normal dualistic mind — our so-called realistic mind — always interprets that something is not right, something is not complete, about me and my surroundings. It is always criticizing. That is the symptom of the dualistic mind: something is always wrong. Our dualistic mind is either placing extra qualities onto what exists or else is underestimating it; such a nervous, dissatisfied mind never follows the middle way. Whether consciously or not it feels, 'My nature is impure. I was born with impurities, right now I am impure, I am going to die with impurities and end up in hell!' It doesn't matter if we call ourselves religious or non-religious, philosophical or atheistic; as long as we are out of touch with basic reality we remain under the influence of such deluded, self-defeating views. If we want to be free of all diseases of body and mind it is extremely important to rid ourselves of all such mistaken, self-pitying concepts.

What is our problem? It is that we feel, 'I am the worst

kind of person: impure, full of hatred, ignorant and greedy. I am so bad!' This kind of thinking — holding such a low opinion of ourselves, even if we do not express it in words — is completely negative. This is what we need to purify.

Tantra says that human beings have a truly divine quality. The nucleus of each human being, each person's essential nature, is something divine, something pure. To realize this, and to make this realization an integral part of our life and not a mere intellectualization, it is necessary, as we have already discussed, to emanate strongly as a deity.

Emanating yourself as a deity has nothing to do with a particular culture or a particular set of beliefs. You are already emanating. When you emanate your self-pity image you do not think that you are involved with a particular culture; you just do it. So stop following this ignorant habit; cultivate strong divine pride and emanate yourself as a deity instead. Begin to live up to your tremendous potential.

The best, most precise way to practise emanating as a deity is to do the three-kaya meditation. The great tantric masters of the past, such as Lama Tzongkhapa, have emphasized that there is nothing more essential than this practice.

DISSOLUTION

The sadhana of the deity we are practising may contain an elaborate description of the three-kaya practice, but it is sufficient to do an abbreviated version such as the following. We start by reminding ourselves of the refuge we have taken in the Three Jewels and cultivating the heartfelt bodhi-citta motivation to achieve enlightenment in order to benefit others. Then we engage in guru-yoga, the root of the tantric path. We visualize our tantric master before us and see him or her as the embodiment of all the enlightened qualities we wish to realize within ourselves. We imagine that the guru comes to the top of our head, dissolves into light and descends into our heart. As the guru sinks into us in this way, we visualize that we are experiencing the various visions of death that lead up to the dawning of the very subtle clear light consciousness. In this way we meditate upon the unification of our guru's blissful wisdom with our own very subtle mind. Drawing upon our memory of the initiations we have received and upon our contact with the guru's clarity and compassion, we should imagine this unification to be as blissful as possible. The more we are able to experience bliss, the better it will be for the process of transformation.

This subtle, blissful experience of union is beyond any of our ordinary dualistic concepts. As all our ordinary appearances dissolve into the empty space of non-dual wisdom and simultaneous great bliss, we concentrate upon this dissolution as single-pointedly as possible. We should think, 'This is the enlightened truth body (dharmakaya) and this is who I really am.' By identifying ourselves as completely as possible with the dharmakaya, we transform the ordinary death experience into the path to enlightenment.

As we meditate upon the dharmakaya in this way, the self-concepts we have been holding onto will break down somewhat; this is good enough to qualify as an actual emptiness experience. Don't become discouraged and think 'I don't have any realization of emptiness. I don't even understand the word emptiness or how to practise anything!' Don't think this way; it is only a hindrance. After all, to some extent we do already have some experience of the clear light. We have died many times in the past and tantra explains that the process of dying antomatically involves the discovery of the clear light and the non-dual nature of totality. Not only while dying but during sleep and orgasm as well we get a taste of this clear light totality. To a certain extent these experiences break down the concrete concepts of the self-pitying mind, softening them somehow. So do not worry about how profound your understanding of emptiness should be; it is enough for the moment that you are no longer involved with the concrete concepts of this and that. Just let go and allow all your grasping to dissolve into clear spaciousness.

Remain alert and feel that this alert consciousness is the wisdom embracing the universal expanse of clean clear space. In this space the self-pitying me, crying and complaining about this and that, is nowhere to be found; it is completely non-existent. Allow the mind to stay in this spaciousness, which is free of all relative puzzles and all false functions, recognizing it as the actual dharmakaya experience. It is a clean clear natural state without even a speck of rubbish thinking, completely empty of all complicated ego conflicts. It is reality and you merely allow your mind to dwell there alertly.

Perhaps you feel uncomfortable with this explanation of the clear light experience. Intellectually you might argue, 'Wait a minute, Thubten Yeshe! If you are saying that emptiness is nothing but the emptiness of space, you are wrong. You have over-simplified a very complex subject. This is not Nagarjuna's view; this is not the Madhyamika philosophy. True emptiness is not the same as merely pretending to dissolve into space.'

You can argue in this way. You can debate all the fine philosophical points and prove that dissolving into space is *not* what is meant by emptiness — but actually this is a garbage argument. Why? Because such an intellectual approach to emptiness often becomes an obstacle to discovering the actual experience of emptiness. You can write a whole book conclusively refuting emptiness-as-space, or argue and debate for an entire lifetime, but it would be a complete waste of time.

It is true that in our studies we try to gain as philosophically correct a view of emptiness as we can so that we can understand it exactly as Nagarjuna and all the other great scholar-meditators have understood it. But *now*, during this meditation, we are not concerned with studying and analyzing; we are concerned with *acting*. And in the context of actualizing the dharmakaya clear light experience, all Indian and Tibetan gurus have stated that space is the number one example for comprehending non-duality, or emptiness.

To gain the true emptiness experience you have to begin somewhere. You have to have some experience, some taste of what it is like to go beyond the mundane, ego-generated puzzles of this and that. This is the main point. Somehow we have to let go of all the gross, concrete and limiting concepts keeping us trapped in an unsatisfactory, mundane view of ourselves and everything else.

From a philosophical point of view, it is said that in emptiness there are no forms, no sounds, no smells and so forth. Such a view can be translated into actual experience by allowing everything to dissolve into space by means of the death process absorptions. In that moment of dissolution your mind has no way to magnetize contact with the accustomed sensory world. In the clear light space of emptiness there are no colours, odours, sensations and so on. All narrow dualistic puzzles disappear and, as a result, the natural state of your mind is allowed to radiate, to embrace the entire world of reality. You stay as long as you can in this spacious, non-dualistic state, and feel that by doing so you have reached the actual dharmakaya: the completely unobscured wisdom of full enlightenment.

REAPPEARANCE

Now, how do you move to the sambhogakaya experience? While floating in the space of the dharmakaya you let go until there is nothing left to disturb your mind. Nothing at all. Then, after some time, the puzzles of relativity will start to reassert themselves, somehow beginning to magnetize your mind, drawing your attention to them. This is the time for you to move from the dharmakaya to the sambhogakaya experience. Only you can know when; no one else can tell what is going on in your mind.

When this dualistic shaking arises in your mind, remember your compassionate wish to benefit others and make the strong determination to arise in a form to which others can relate. Then within the space of non-duality — the clear light space of emptiness — something begins to appear. This is like a small cloud suddenly appearing in the expanse of clear sky. The shape and the colour of what appears in the spaciousness of your mind at this point depends upon the type of practice you are doing. In many sadhanas it is a syllable or letter symbolizing the main deity. Or it can be a squiggle, or a seed, or some other shape. But.whatever it is should be understood as a subtle manifestation of your consciousness itself. It is not something that you are watching from the outside; instead, you should feel completely unified with it. It is the shape of your own emerging mind.

Then, just as you strongly identified the spacious clear light as the actual dharmakaya experience, you should now recognize this subtle, transparent form — which is similar to the immaterial body we possess when in the ordinary bardo between death and birth — as the actual sambhogakaya experience. It, too, should be experienced as the indistinguishable unity of great bliss and non-dual wisdom, now identified as the actual enjoyment body (sambhogakaya) of a buddha. Think: 'This is the real sambhogakaya; it is who I really am.' For a while maintain the clear appearance of this seed-syllable and the divine pride of being the sambhogakaya, thereby transforming the ordinary intermediate state experience into the path of the enlightened enjoyment body.

When you are ready, bring to mind your bodhicitta motivation to work for the sake of others and make the strong determination to arise in a form to which even more beings can relate. With this compassionate motive the seed-syllable suddenly transforms into the transparent rainbow body of the deity itself. Understand this as being the actual emanation body (nirmanakaya) of full awakening that replaces the gross physical body of ordinary rebirth and has the nature of simultaneous bliss and wisdom. Once again, identify strongly with this appearance by thinking, This is the real nirmanakaya; it is who I really am.' In this way, then, ordinary rebirth is taken into the path as the emana- tion body of a buddha.

When you see yourself as a deity, you should feel that you are the real emanation of the deity. Don't think that you are just pretending; you should be convinced. Then, like the actor who remains in character even after the play is finish- ed, you might surprise yourself to find that you have actual- ly become the deity. Such divine pride — the strong sense of actually being the deity — is crucial. With it, tantric trans- formation will come naturally and be very powerful. Those people who think that tantra is only involved with *pretend- ing* to be a deity are completely mistaken.

LETTING GO

Although during your meditation you may be trying your best to stay in a conscious, open state of non-duality, you may easily become distracted by the arisal of various super- stitious thoughts. When this happens, instead of fighting with these superstitions it is often best to simply imagine yourself strongly as your particular deity — as Tara, for example — and develop a deep awareness of great love and compassion. Stay within the space of this deep awareness and just let yourself *be* Tara.

If again you find yourself distracted by concepts of this and that — suddenly you are thinking about eating a pizza! — do not give them a lot of energy. Instead of entering into conversation in your mind — 'How I wish I had a pizza! Instead of sitting here miserably in meditation I could be enjoying myself' — start to say Tara's mantra, *om tara tuttare ture svaha*, until you settle down again. This is much more skilful than letting yourself get carried away by the worldly mantra, *pizza, pizza, pizza*.

Too much expectation is another great hindrance to suc- cessful meditation. This superstitious attitude prevents us from being satisfied with our meditational experiences and continually forces us to compare these experiences with some imagined ideal. We upset ourselves by thinking, 'According to the teachings I have received, at this point I should be experiencing great bliss, but what I am feeling now is hardly blissful. I must be a failure!' We make ourselves so tense anticipating the expected experience that it never comes. This is easily understandable; how can bliss ever arise in a mind that is worried and uptight?

The only solution is to *let go*. Realize that expectations are a hindrance and let go of them as soon as they arise. In other words, we should be a little looser in our approach. Sometimes we put too much energy into our practice or we discipline ourselves too severely, thinking that this will bring us more quickly to the desired realizations. But too much effort often has the opposite effect; it prevents our progress instead of helping it.

Think of new drivers who have not yet learned to relax behind the wheel. Because they are anxious to do everything correctly they are constantly busy, adjusting their steering, speed and so forth. The result is a jerky, uncomfortable ride. Instead of being a pleasurable experience, driving becomes a chore. Experienced drivers, on the other hand, are relaxed. Although they remain aware of what is going on, they have learned to let go and allow the car to drive itself. As a result their ride is smooth and effortless and it sometimes feels as if the car were flying blissfully through the air rather than bouncing noisily along the road! If we want to experience a similar bliss in meditation, we must learn to let go of our expectations and decrease our excessive, self-conscious efforts.

DIVINE PRIDE AND CLEAR APPEARANCE

The generation stage training in the divine pride of a deity is very important. Our normal tendency is to feel dissatisfied and to criticize our body, speech and mind. 'My body is out of shape; my voice is unpleasant; my mind is confused.'

We are so caught up in this pointless, neurotic habit of criti-
cism that we disparage others as well as ourselves. From the
tantric point of view this is extremely damaging.

The way to counter this tendency is to cultivate a sense of
divine pride, the strong feeling when entering the nirmanakaya experience, for example, that you are the *actual* fully
enlightened emanation body of a buddha, that your mind is
completely free of all superstitions, all limitations. Otherwise, if you continue to hold onto the idea that you are
basically confused and angry, you will manifest as a confused
and angry person, certainly not as a blissful deity. You can stop
this destructive way of thinking about yourself and avoid
the negative, self-defeating consequences by concentrating
on the oneness of your own fundamental consciousness and
the wise, compassionate qualities of the guru-deity. In this
way you open yourself up to the great waves of inspiration
that can transform your life completely. The more intensely
you concentrate on this feeling of divine pride, the more
profoundly will you experience freedom from all forms of
limitation and dissatisfaction.

The practice of highest yoga tantra — rather like an
excellent Christmas pudding, which is rich, wholesome and
quite delicious – should have three special flavours: one, the
appearance of oneself and of all other beings should be that
of the deity; two, one's mind should be inseparable from
nondual wisdom; and three, every experience should be of
great bliss, great joy.

Don't just *pretend* to be the deity, Heruka for example, as I
have already said. That is not what you are doing when you
visualize yourself as the deity. Instead, you should feel from
the depths of your being that you *are* Heruka, that you and
he are an inseparable unity. The more you cultivate this
unity, the more powerful your experience of transformation
will become. This is completely natural.

You should also practise seeing all appearances as illusory, lacking concreteness as something 'out there' separate
from your mind. In other words, you should recognize all
appearances as arising from emptiness, as having the very

nature of emptiness, of non-duality. Finally, your experience of empty, illusory appearance should be of an exceedingly blissful nature. This is accomplished during the completion stage of highest yoga tantra by bringing your attention inside in such a way that you become intensely aware of the blissful kundalini energy pervading your nervous system. This enables you to blend all your experiences with this great blissful energy.

As an aid to the process of transformation, certain physical exercises, such as those contained in hatha-yoga, play a very important part in the practice of the completion stage. But they are not merely exercises designed to improve our posture or better our health. Their ultimate purpose is to increase our blissful kundalini energy. This blissful energy pervades our entire nervous system, but the problem is that we don't recognize it. Through the proper practice of hatha-yoga we can learn to get in touch with and even increase this blissful energy and learn how to communicate with it so that we can bring it anywhere we want to. This is not for the purpose of gaining ordinary pleasure but rather to gain control over the subtlest levels of our body and mind.

However, when performing any of these exercises it is essential to maintain mindfulness of oneself as a deity. We must put away our limited self-image and all our self-pitying ideas, for only then will these exercises become truly effective. Through proper practice there will come a time when merely touching a part of our body will cause great bliss to arise. As the body starts feeling lighter and more flexible, physical energies that before were a source of pain begin to activate sensations of extreme pleasure. Tantric transformation, then, is not merely a matter of imagination; our physical being is profoundly transformed as well.

THE TANTRIC PERSONALITY

Many people say, 'The body is not really important; the most important thing is to meditate inwardly.' But this is wrong. According to tantra we cannot say that the mind is more important than the body or that the body is more important than the mind. They are of equal importance. In tantric practice the body is understood to be like a plot of ground containing untold mineral wealth. This body of ours, for all its suffering nature, contains the most valuable of natural resources: kundalini gold, kundalini oil!

At one time or another we have all experienced sensations of great bodily bliss. Sometimes we are just sitting down relaxing and suddenly a feeling of intense bliss will sweep over us. This experience is common and is not a particularly high realization. But it does give a hint of the great store of blissful energy contained within our body even at the present moment. The purpose of the various yogas, exercises and meditations of highest tantra is to arouse, control and utilize this blissful energy resource for the attainment of complete fulfilment: the enlightenment of buddhahood. For as long as you do not lose your head and can maintain mindfulness, it does not matter how much blissful pleasure you have. It does not matter whether you call this pleasure samsaric, worldly or whatever — it can lead to liberation.

The essence of tantra is dealing skilfully with pleasure. The person who qualifies for tantra is someone who can cope with pleasure, someone for whom dealing with pleasure becomes a conducive situation for achieving liberation. This is the tantric personality. If a person only knows how to be miserable then tantra will not work for him or her. Like a nuclear reactor without any fuel, such a person will have no resource to utilize for the necessary transformations.

However, the resource of pleasure is already existent within this human body of ours. This is one major reason why this human form is considered so precious. What we need is a skilful method for awakening and then using this resource to bring perfect happiness not only to ourselves but to all others as well. In order to do this, we must learn to break the habit of relating to our experiences in life with a miserable mind, with our accustomed miserable projections. We should recognize that we create all human problems ourselves. We should not blame them on society; we should not blame our mother and father or our friends; we should not blame anyone else. Our problems are our own creation. But just as we are the creator of all our own problems we are also the creator of our own liberation, and everything that is necessary for attaining this blissful liberation is contained in the body and mind we have right at this very moment.

INTEGRATING WISDOM AND ENJOYMENT

The purpose of generating ourselves as a deity through the practice of the three bodies, or kayas, of a buddha is to smash through our self-pitying concept, our suffocating conception of ego. For it is this limiting conceptualization that prevents us from experiencing the explosion of blissful energy latent within our nervous system and thereby realizing our potential for full enlightenment.

The wisdom of emptiness is blissful. It is very important that two elements — clear-sighted wisdom into the true nature of things and the feeling of joyous blissfulness — be unified in one experience. In the West we can see that while so many young people are intelligent they still experience very little or no joy in their lives. Being smart has not made them happy. Instead, many of them are totally disturbed. They can accomplish all sorts of feats, such as designing complex computer games, but because they lack the proper methods for integrating their intellect and their emotions they remain dry, intellectual, sterile and very dissatisfied.

In contrast, there are other people who have a more practical ability to enjoy themselves. But many of them have no clear intelligence, no sharp penetrating awareness. Although they have a certain contentment in their lives, their minds are dull and plodding.

Tantra tries to cultivate great wisdom, putting intelligence into practical experience, by unifying it with blissfully heightened awareness. In this way it is possible to integrate one's life and fulfil one's potential for happiness while eradicating all the problems normally associated with the pursuit of pleasure. For in this world pleasure *is* a problem. For many affluent people gross physical miseries such as hunger and disease are not really a significant problem at all. But how to deal with pleasure without becoming berserk or degenerate — that is a big unanswered question for them. The unified tantric experience offers the solution.

It has already been mentioned several times that according to tantra, the fundamental human problem is that when we have pleasure we generally become more ignorant, more dark inside. This does not mean we should not have pleasure. We *should* have pleasure, but we need to keep from going out of control while experiencing pleasure. We have to keep from falling under the influence of ignorance and delusion. So at this time we are learning how it is possible to experience incredible pleasure while remaining in a state of clarity and control. We are learning how the experience of pleasure can give rise to clean clear penetrative wisdom.

It is common for us to be possessive about what is happening to us. Even when we are successful in our meditations and feel the blissful kundalini energy arising, there is a strong tendency to hold onto it tightly: This is *my* experience; it is *mine!*' This is the habit we have to break somehow. We must learn to allow pleasurable experiences to happen without grabbing onto them as *mine.* We can accomplish this by unifying our mind with emptiness, with non-duality. Then when pleasure arises it is as if it is being experienced somewhere out in space. It is difficult to express this in words so I hope you don't have trouble understanding what I am trying to say. Somehow, we have to go beyond our normal habit of possessiveness, of relating everything to our limited sense of self.

Perhaps I can make it a little clearer. Imagine that in front of you is a person, a man or a woman, whom you find extremely attractive. Just looking at this person arouses great energy in you. Maybe you want to reach out and grab him or her. Now imagine that this person suddenly dissolves into rainbow light, radiant and transparent. Automatically all your heavy feelings of desire and possessiveness also dissolve and in their place something lighter, more buoyant arises. You still have some relationship with this beautiful object but it has changed. You have let go of your grasping attitude and now experience something more spacious, more universal, instead. It is such a light, blissful, yet intensely aware experience that I am talking about. This is what we are trying to cultivate.

12   *Final Accomplishment*

THE COMPLETION STAGE: INNER FIRE AND ENERGY CONTROL

The generation stage practice of the three kayas is in fact only a rehearsal for the more advanced completion stage practices that actually transform our ordinary body and mind into the completely transcendent body and mind of an enlightened being. But the generation stage preparation is absolutely necessary: it is only through loosening the concrete concepts we have about ourselves — by generating the clear appearance of the deity out of the space of emptiness and cultivating strong divine pride that we are the actual deity — that we create the room needed for the transformations to take place.

Once we are skilled enough to engage in the completion stage practices, such as generating the inner heat (Tibetan: *tum-mo*) at our navel centre, we will be able to bring all our energy winds into the central channel and cause them to dissolve into it completely, as they do at death. As a result the clear light wisdom of our fundamental mind will actually dawn, and eventually we will be able to manifest the rainbow-like illusory body, which can leave and return to our old physical body at will. These things actually happen; they are not mere visualizations anymore, as they were during the generation stage. The precious kundalini energy dormant within us is actually aroused; we attain the simultaneously born great blissful wisdom; and we overcome the limitations of our ordinary physical form.

When we gain control over our internal wind energy to such an extent that we can direct it into whichever channel we choose, we will also be able to control the external wind energy as well. There are many stories that illustrate the great influence highly accomplished tantric meditators have had over the external elements. For example, at one of the great prayer festivals organized by Je Tzongkhapa in Lhasa, thousands of butter lamps were lit as offerings before the statue of Shakyamuni Buddha. At a certain point the fire got out of control and the people, in panic, ran to Lama Tzongkhapa shouting: 'Your offerings are going to burn down the temple!' So he sat down, went into deep meditative absorption, and suddenly all the butter lamps stopped burning. People may call this a miracle, but in fact there is nothing mysterious or unexplainable about it. Someone with the great mastery over his or her internal energies that Tzongkhapa undoubtedly possessed can definitely manipulate external energy as well.

I think that the inner fire meditation is perfectly suited to the Western mentality. Why? Because the Western mind is fascinated by material: people love to work with material, play with material, fix material and transform material. And by manipulating material they try to manipulate people's minds as well. Tum-mo meditation tries to do the same thing: by manipulating the energy within our physical form it enables us to expand the range of our consciousness and experience advanced levels of blissful wisdom.

It also seems to me that many Westerners are extremely impatient; they want instant results. They buy instant coffee, instant soup, instant breakfast, instant everything. And when it comes to the spiritual path they want instant satisfaction, instant experiences. With the inner fire meditation, that is what we get. By following certain simple, practical steps − all of which are precisely and scientifically laid out − we get the results: a completely transformed state of conscious awareness. We do not have to adopt any unusual religious beliefs; we just follow the instructions and the experiences come automatically. By concentrating on the energies existing within our own body and mind, we bring about a profound change in the reality we experience. It is so simple and direct, so straightforward.

This twentieth century is incredibly fast, so full of energy. With this tremendous explosion of energy many good things are happening and many destructive things as well. This is how it is. Therefore, if we want to do something positive with our life, we need a method that is at least as powerful as the confused, materialistic energies we are caught up in. Philosophical ideas, no matter how grand, are just not strong enough to help us out of our present crises. By themselves, such ideas are as insubstantial as clouds; they may look convincing at first but they quickly evaporate, leaving us as helpless as before. What we need is something active, something powerful, something direct. We need something we can act upon *now* and get results from *now*. This 'something' is tantra, especially the completion stage practice of tum-mo.

All this talk about instant results and the generation of incredible bliss sounds attractive, but we should not forget two very important points. First of all, although tum-mo practice definitely leads to the experience of bliss, its primary purpose is to enable us to enter into a state of clear light wisdom. It is this wisdom − a clear insight into the true nature of reality − that frees us from the bondage of our delusions. Bliss by itself cannot do this. Therefore, throughout tum-mo meditation we must develop as strong a comprehension as possible of emptiness, of non-duality, of the non-self-existent nature of the blissful experience itself. If we follow our old habits and relate to the blissful feelings as if they were concrete and self-existent, tum-mo meditation's powerful production of desirous energy will lead to disastrous results.

Furthermore, we should never be so carried away by our pursuit of bliss that we forget the motivation behind the entire practice of tantra. The ultimate aim of the buddhist path, of both sutra and tantra, is to be of maximum benefit to others. If we become so caught up in striving for the experience of bliss that we neglect dedicating ourselves to the welfare of others, there is absolutely no way we can ever be successful in our practices. All we will be doing is creating the causes for yet more unhappiness and frustration.

BLISSFUL AWARENESS

As we become more and more familiar with the blissful experience of clear light available within our central channel, we will be developing a powerful method for transcending the ordinary, limited experiences of this sensory world. We will be able to unify whatever occurs to us during our daily life with this inner experience of blissful awareness. There is no longer any danger that the ordinary pleasures we experience will disturb the tranquility of our mind. Instead, whatever sensory pleasure we experience through contacting desirous objects will be blended effortlessly with blissful wisdom and will therefore only serve to increase our inner peace.

Whenever any one of our sense organs contacts a pleasure-giving object, instead of descending into our habitual pattern of grasping, attachment, dullness and disappointment, we will be able to channel the desirous energy that is aroused so that it embraces our entire nervous system. And at the same time we will be able to allow this emerging, blissful consciousness to become absorbed indistinguishably into the clear space of non-duality. All the old problems associated with desire will have been solved; instead of being the cause of dissatisfaction, desire is now fuelling the experience of totality.

With the development of our internal source of bliss and satisfaction we will find ourselves making fewer and fewer emotional demands on our surroundings. Our inner clarity will gradually liberate us from dependence upon outer circumstances. If things in the external world are not working out well, this ceases to be a problem for us. We also stop being anxious about the future; why worry about missing out on some transitory pleasure tomorrow when we already have a supply of bliss within ourselves right at this present moment? And do not think that this inner experience of bliss is somehow selfish. The more internally satisfied we are, the more we can give pleasure and satisfaction to others.

Of course, training our mind to behave in such a liberated way requires a lot of practice. At the moment it is not easy for us to cultivate and maintain this sense of inner satisfaction and balance. But by remembering those times in our life when we did experience some measure of calm satisfaction, we can develop confidence in our ability to experience such inner peace again. And especially when we have been introduced to the profound tantric techniques for generating unimaginable bliss and clarity of mind, we will have good reason for feeling inspired. The more we train ourselves in these techniques, the more we will realize that it is definitely possible to make our life truly worthwhile for both ourselves and others.

DAKAS AND DAKINIS

When the completion stage practices have been mastered and we have gained control over our subtle energy winds and so forth, there will come a time when the dakas and dakinis will come. What are dakas and dakinis? Simply speaking, they are males and females who possess advanced experiences of tantric transformation and control and are therefore able to increase the blissful wisdom of a highly qualified practitioner. There is a certain point in the mastery of the completion stage when physically embracing such a consort is necessary for bringing all the pervading energy winds into the central channel, a prerequisite for opening the heart centre completely and experiencing the profoundest level of clear light.

This subject of practice with a consort is open to great

misinterpretation, especially by people who have made only superficial contact with buddhist tantra. Many Westerners, for instance, because they have seen Tibetan paintings and statues showing deities in embrace, have the mistaken notion that Tibetan Buddhism is mainly concerned with sexual contact between men and women. As was pointed out earlier, what this art is actually representing is the experience of total unity — of method and wisdom, bliss and emptiness — characteristic of the fully enlightened state. But now with the mention of the completion stage practices there is a further opportunity for confusion to arise. Therefore it should be emphasized that until we have gained mastery over our subtle body and have 'embraced' the blissful kundalini energy dormant within, we are not at all qualified to embrace an external consort.

There are vast differences between tantric embrace and ordinary sexual contact. How different these two are becomes clear when we remember that at the time of the completion stage the practitioner has dissolved the energy winds into his or her central channel, thereby experiencing the same mental and physical absorptions occurring at the time of death. Unless these death-like experiences have been entered into with full consciousness and control, it is a farce to talk about tantric embrace. Moreover, while in ordinary sex it is the man who enters the woman's body, in true tantric embrace it is the woman's energy that penetrates the man!

THE FRUIT OF TANTRIC PRACTICE

We should realize that there are various degrees of success to be attained by following these tantric techniques of transformation. The highest accomplishment, of course, would be to achieve the three actual bodies of a buddha — that is, complete enlightenment — before death, in this very lifetime. This is definitely possible. There are many accomplished practitioners who have attained full awakening in just this way. Yet even if we cannot uncover the totality of our being now, it is still possible to do so at the actual time of death, or even in the intermediate state between lives. And even if our practices fail to lead us all the way to enlightenment, they can still free us from the fears of death and give us some measure of control over our rebirth. This itself would be a great accomplishment for it would allow us to continue our spiritual journey uninterruptedly in the future.

When you enter into any meditational practice, no matter how difficult it may appear at first, you should try to be brave and think, 'Whether I am completely successful or not, at least I'll try to gain *some* experience.' Do not feel, 'How can I meditate? I'm new to this and know nothing about meditation. Besides, I have created so much negativity in my life; I'm such a sinful person. How can someone like me ever hope to gain realizations?' This way of thinking is completely mistaken. First of all, you never know what your level of attainment can be until you try. Because you are obscured at the moment, you do not know what your true potential is. If you try your best you may surprise yourself. Secondly, it is foolish to worry that you are too sinful to be able to meditate successfully. Look at Milarepa. He created so much negativity, killing so many people, yet he had the strength to win perfect realization of renunciation, bodhicitta and emptiness, finally attaining complete enlightenment through the practice of tantra. Although, as he himself admitted, he was once a great criminal, through the guidance of his guru Marpa and his own determination he was able to channel his energy and become a great and most successful meditator. If he was able to overcome his negative past, why do you think you are trapped by yours, which is so mild in comparison?

Also, I have noticed that the people who have created

heavy negativities in their lives are often the most successful when they turn to spiritual matters, while those who put little energy into samsara often put little energy into gaining nirvana as well. They are too numb to accomplish anything, good or bad.

My point in mentioning all this is that, as a human being, you should never set a limit on how much you can accomplish, no matter what your life has been like so far. It could be that your attempts at meditation have been full of distraction, and suddenly some potential ripens, giving you the surprising ability to concentrate uninterruptedly for long periods of time. These things definitely do happen, so be brave and keep trying. At the very least you should make the strong determination: 'I am going to gain enough control over my mind so that if disaster strikes, or when I die, I shall have the concentration and clarity to remain calm and recognize what is happening.' If you can maintain just this type of motivation for your practice, that is sufficient. It will keep alive the possibility of fulfilling your inner potential, which is much greater than you probably think.

QUALITIES LEADING TO SUCCESS

If we are to attain *any* level of realization through tantric practice, however, there are four qualities we must possess. The first is *indestructible devotion*. This means having a clear understanding that the path we are following, from taking refuge in the beginning to actualizing the most advanced tantric methods at the end, is reliable and worthwhile. Once we see from our own experience that we can entrust ourselves to this path, because it does in fact lead us in the direction we want to go, then our devotion to it will naturally become indestructible.

To put it in another way, we need to have confidence in what we are doing. This is easy as long as we are in the company of other meditators and practitioners or near our teacher. In such a protected environment spiritual practice is like a shared culture; it is something we can have faith in and follow without feeling strange or out-of-place. But when we leave this artificially isolated situation and return to the 'real' world, we can quickly lose confidence in our practice. We feel the pressure of people's expectations and values — 'What is the point of meditating? Why sit around and contemplate your navel when there are so many other exciting things to do with your life?' — and can easily fall under their influence. Soon we find ourselves submerged once again in the habitual garbage of everyday life, with no means for changing it into anything worthwhile. But if our confidence is unshakeable then our devotion to our practices will also be unshakeable, and instead of being swept away by external circumstances we will be able to transform them into the path.

The second quality we need is to be *free from doubt*, the indecisiveness that results from having an unclear mind. When we develop the clear wisdom that understands the various elements of the practice, their order, their purpose and so forth, all the crippling doubts preventing us from following the path with firm determination will vanish automatically.

It is important for us to be as aware as possible of the firm structure holding our practices together. There are many people who have listened to a great deal of dharma teachings for many years and sometimes I hear them complain, 'I am so confused I don't know where to begin. I have received teachings from so many lamas that I no longer know who my main teacher is; I don't even know which meditation to do first.' If we have studied many different subjects, have received many different initiations, have been introduced to many different meditations and *still* do not know how to practise, this shows that we have lost sight of the structure underlying the practice. One of the beautiful things about the Tibetan buddhist tradition — please excuse my chauvinism — is that there exists within it a clean clear structure from the beginning to the end. There is a checklist, as it were, of attainments, realizations and so forth. From my point of view this is to be appreciated very much. Therefore if you feel lost, check for yourself, with the aid of an experienced guide, what this structure is and then follow it in a steadily progressive way.

Thirdly, it is important to develop *one-pointed concentration*. It will be impossible to penetrate to the depths of the practice and taste its essence if our concentration lacks stability and focus. For example, if we want to gain control over the different energies within our subtle nervous system, we cannot be content with a vague, imprecise idea about where these energies are and how they are functioning. Instead, we have to have as accurate an understanding as we can, and this is only possible if we have a concentrated mind. In this respect tantra is no different from any other discipline. The people who are successful in what they do — whether it is in academic studies, sport or whatever — all have one thing in common: well-developed concentration. Without it one cannot get very far.

Consider the following example. It has been said many times that through the practice of tantra all activity motivated by desire — even drinking a milk shake — can be transformed into the experience of great blissful wisdom. If our concentration is strong and we have trained ourselves well, we can follow exactly what is happening as we taste and swallow the milk shake. All the energy that is aroused can be channeled so that it increases the inner fire at the navel. This heat sends much blissful energy into the nervous system and the entire experience becomes flavoured by the spacious wisdom of non-duality. For the person who knows what he or she is doing, simply drinking a milk shake becomes a powerful method for touching the reality of blissful wisdom. It is not a matter of wishing or pretending; this actually happens.

But normally we are out of touch with our inner reality.

When we drink something, for instance, we have no direct awareness of what is happening in our tongue, stomach, nervous system or body and mind in general. Unlike the yogi or yogini who knows exactly what is happening and can manipulate the energy this way and that if necessary, we remain dull and unaware. Then, instead of blissful wisdom perhaps all we experience is diarrhoea.

Lastly, if we wish to attain the highest realization we should *keep our practices hidden*. This may sound peculiar but it is actually a very important point. In fact, the correct term for the practice of tantra is 'secret mantra.' Here, 'mantra' means protection of the mind and 'secret' is a reminder that these powerful methods should be kept to ourselves, like a precious treasure. These days the practice of tantra has become quite degenerate; some people following a particular practice openly boast, 'I am a tantrika! Listen to what I can do!' Such proud, public behaviour is unwise; it only attracts hindrances to our practice. It is far better to retain a subdued outer appearance and be a great yogi inwardly than it is to make a big show on the outside but have no realizations within.

The great meditators of the past have said that if we cultivate these four causes — indestructible devotion, freedom from doubt, single-pointedness and secrecy — and practise steadily and correctly, then all the powerful attainments of the path are definitely within our reach. According to the experience of many practitioners, we can reach a certain point in our meditational training when a great explosion of knowledge and realization occurs. It is as if before we were an ordinary, ignorant being and suddenly we are transformed into a highly realized yogi! This is not a Tibetan religious fantasy; it actually happens.

As ordinary human beings we are wrapped tightly in blankets of superstition. If we can somehow let go of these smothering concepts, we can cut through to an unbelievably profound dimension of reality immediately. Even though we are not expecting anything special to happen, suddenly this great explosion of realization takes place, effortlessly and spontaneously. This is definitely possible. But it is no use merely reading about the experiences of others; if we want to receive the benefits of tantric transformation, we must cultivate the experiences ourselves.

Afterword

Despite the debilitating effect of his deteriorating heart condition, Lama Yeshe continued up until the very end of his life to display more concern for those around him than he did for himself. Even while he was undergoing intensive care in the hospital he would inquire about the health and welfare of others and would laugh and joke with his nurses. Then, as Lama Zopa Rinpoche has reported, 'Shortly before he passed away, when surgery was being contemplated, he told me, "It doesn't matter whether the operation is successful or not for I have been able to use myself as a servant to others. I am completely satisfied with what I have done and not at all upset about dying."' Finally, on the Tibetan New Year, Lama Yeshe departed, his breathing having stopped at the dawn hour when many great yogis have passed away.

Expressions such as 'passed away' and 'departed' are usually little more than euphemisms employed to soften the grim finality of death. But here they have a special significance, for according to the tantric teachings just presented, death is not the total annihilation that some people fear it is. Rather, it is a stage in the progressive refinement of consciousness that continues until the mind achieves its greatest possible subtlety, after which it departs, leaving the body behind. While the body then begins to disintegrate, the mind continues on, eventually meeting the appropriate conditions for the next embodiment, or incarnation.

As Lama Yeshe explained, if a person has not prepared

sufficiently, this movement from one life to the next takes place without control or choice and one dies and is reborn in the same state of ignorantly conditioned grasping and aversion in which he or she had previously lived. But for the well-trained bodhisattva the situation is very different. With clear-minded, conscious control, such an altruistically motivated person takes full advantage of death's blissfully subtle clear light consciousness and — always guided by the compassionate intention to be of greatest benefit — chooses a rebirth that will allow him or her to continue serving others.

This was the case with Lama Yeshe's death. Not only did he maintain a peaceful and cheerful composure that was extraordinary for someone in his dire physical condition but he was able to remain conscious and fully in control throughout the death process and beyond.

Barely an hour before he died, on March 3, 1984, Lama Yeshe asked Zopa Rinpoche, who had been with him constantly, to practise Heruka meditation with him. Then, just before dawn, his heart stopped beating and, according to Western medical interpretation, he was considered dead. But Lama's mind had not yet left his body, and he continued to meditate undisturbed — despite at least two hours of intensive effort on the part of the doctor in charge to resuscitate him.

Eventually, he was moved to another room in the hospital where he remained in the most subtle state of meditation, with Rinpoche and many of his students present, for most of the day. At around five in the afternoon one of the people thought he noticed Lama's head move slightly but felt he must have been hallucinating. However, just then Rinpoche turned to him and said quietly, 'Now Lama's meditation is finished.' At that moment Lama Yeshe's mind had finally left his body.

On February 12, 1985, just under a year later, a boy was born to a Spanish couple with whom, as Lama Yeshe himself had said years before, he shared a special relation-

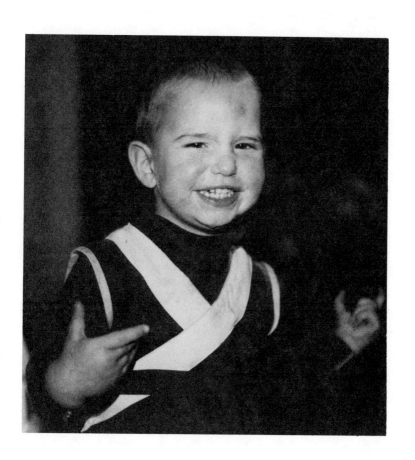

ship; this couple lived and worked at the Ösel Ling Retreat Centre that Lama Yeshe had founded in Spain, near Granada. The child was named Ösel, meaning Clear Light, and by the time he was fourteen months old he had been recognized as the reincarnation of Lama Yeshe, not only by Zopa Rinpoche but by His Holiness the Dalai Lama as well. At the time of formal recognition the Dalai Lama declared that when young Ösel was old enough to speak well he would give unmistakable indications that he was indeed the true reincarnation, or tulku, of Lama Yeshe. Since then, people from all over the world have had the chance to meet young Lama Ösel and already he has displayed to many of them − including those who had been extremely sceptical about rebirth − remarkable signs, such as recognizing people and places from his former life. Lama Ösel was enthroned, amid extensive media attention, in Dharamsala, India, on March 17, 1987.

By returning quickly in response to the heartfelt requests of his former disciples, Lama Yeshe has fulfilled his promise to continue working for others. Not only that, but the manner in which he died and then returned has demonstrated most impressively the validity and power of the teachings presented in this introductory work. May all who are interested find benefit and joy in the teachings of tantric transformation, may Lama Ösel enjoy a long and fruitful life so that he can be of maximum help and inspiration to others, and may all beings be happy.

Glossary

Avalokiteshvara (Tib. Chenrezig) male meditational deity embodying fully enlightened compassion.

awakening enlightenment; an enlightened being's state of having awakened from the sleep of ignorance.

bardo (Tib.) the intermediate state between death and rebirth.

bindu (Skt.) see drops.

bliss an extremely pleasurable feeling; in highest *yoga tantra*, the very subtle clear light mind experiencing great bliss is focused on emptiness.

bodhicitta (Skt.) the altruistic motive of a *bodhisattva*; the wish to attain enlightenment in order to benefit others; the fully open and dedicated heart.

bodhisattva (Skt.) someone whose spiritual practice is directed towards the achievement of enlightenment; one who possesses the compassionate motive of *bodhicitta*.

buddha (Skt.) a fully enlightened being; one who has removed all obscurations veiling the mind and has developed all good qualities to perfection; the first of the three jewels of refuge.

Buddha see Shakyamuni Buddha.

buddhahood see enlightenment.

central channel (SKt. *avadhuti, shushuma*; Tib. *tsa u-ma*) the major energy channel of the *vajra* body, visualized as a hollow tube of light located in front of the spine.

chakra (Skt.) energy-wheel; a focal point of energy along the central channel upon which one's concentration is directed, especially during the completion stage of highest *yoga tantra*.

channels (Skt. *nadi*) a constituent of the *vajra* body through which energy-winds and drops flow.

clear appearance visualization of oneself and one's surround-

ings in the purified form of a meditational deity and *mandala;*
cf. generation stage.

clear light (Tib. *ö-sel*) the very subtlest state of mind, achieved
when all the energy-winds have dissolved into the central
channel as happens during death and the completion stage of
highest *yoga tantra.*

compassion (Skt. *karuna*) the wish for all beings to be separated from their mental and physical suffering; a prerequisite
for the development of *bodhicitta;* symbolized by Avalokiteshvara.

completion stage (Tib. *dzog-rim*) the second of the two stages
of highest *yoga tantra,* during which control is gained over the
vajra body through such practices as inner fire.

concentration the ability to focus the mind on any chosen
object of meditation and keep it there.

cyclic existence see *samsara.*

daka (Skt.) literally, a sky-goer (Tib. *ka-dro*); a male being who
helps arouse blissful energy in a qualified tantric practitioner.

dakini (Skt.) literally, a female sky-goer (Tib. *ka-dro-ma*); a
female being who helps arouse blissful energy in a qualified
tantric practitioner.

Dalai Lama the temporal and spiritual leader of Tibet, recognized as the human embodiment of Avalokiteshvara, the
buddha of compassion; the current Dalai Lama, Tenzin
Gyatso, was born in 1935 and is the fourteenth of his line.

death the separation of the mind from the body at the end of
one's life.

definite emergence (Tib. *nge-jung*) the attitude of wishing to
leave behind the sufferings of *samsara* and their cause and to
attain instead the peace of *nirvana* or the full enlightenment of
buddhahood; commonly referred to as renunciation.

deity-*yoga* the tantric practice of generating oneself in the form
of a meditational deity within purified surroundings.

delusion (Skt. *klesha;* Tib. *nyon-mong*) an obscuration cover-
ing the essentially pure nature of the mind and thereby
responsible for suffering and dissatisfaction; chief among the
delusions is ignorance, out of which desirous attachment,
hatred, jealousy and all the other delusions grow.

dharma (Skt.) spiritual teachings; literally, that which holds
one back from suffering; the second of the three jewels of
refuge.

dharmakaya (Skt.)   see truth body.

divine pride   the strong conviction that one has achieved the state of a particular meditational deity; cf. generation stage.

drops (Skt. *bindu*)   a constituent of the *vajra* body used in the generation of great bliss; of the two types, the red drops are received from one's mother and the white drops from one's father at conception.

dualistic view   ignorant view characteristic of the unenlightened mind in which all things are falsely conceived to have concrete self-existence; to such a view, the appearance of an object is mixed with the false image of its being independent or self-existent, thereby leading to further dualistic views concerning subject and object, self and other, this and that, etc.

ego-grasping (Skt. *atmagraha;* Tib. *dag-dzin*)   the ignorant compulsion to regard one's own personality or 'I' as permanent, self-existent and independent of all other phenomena.

emanation body (Skt. *nirmanakaya*)   form in which the enlightened mind appears in order to benefit ordinary beings; cf. three bodies of a *buddha*.

empowerment (Tib. *wang*)   transmission received from a tantric master allowing a disciple to engage in the practices of a particular meditational deity; also referred to as an initiation.

emptiness (Skt. *shunyata*)   the absence of all false ideas about how things exist; specifically, the lack of the apparent independent, self-existence of phenomena.

emptiness-*yoga*   in buddhist *tantra*, the practice of dissolving all ordinary appearances into emptiness as a prerequisite for arising in the purified form of a meditational deity.

energy-wheel   see *chakra*.

energy-wind (Skt. *prana*)   a constituent of the *vajra* body; the energy serving as the mount for the various gross and subtle states of consciousness.

enjoyment body (Skt. *sambhogakaya*)   form in which the enlightened mind appears in order to benefit highly realized bodhisattvas; cf. three bodies of a *buddha*.

enlightenment (Skt. *bodhi*)   full awakening; buddhahood; the ultimate goal of buddhist practice, attained when all limitations have been removed from the mind and all one's positive potential has been realized; a state characterized by unlimited compassion, skill and wisdom.

equanimity   an even-minded attitude towards everyone, cultivated by overcoming the habit to classify others as either friend, enemy or stranger; the necessary basis for developing the compassionate *bodhicitta* motivation.

four classes of *tantra*   the division of *tantra* into *kriya* (action), *carya* (performance), *yoga* and *anuttara-yoga* (highest yoga).

four noble truths   the subject matter of Shakyamuni Buddha's first discourse, or *sutra;* namely, (1) suffering, (2) the cause of suffering, (3) the cessation of suffering and (4) the path leading to this cessation.

generation stage (Tib. *kye-rim*)   the first of the two stages of highest *yoga tantra,* during which one cultivates the clear appearance and divine pride of one's chosen meditational deity.

graded path (Tib. *lam-rim*)   a presentation of Shakyamuni Buddha's teachings in a form suitable for the step-by-step training of a disciple.

guru (Skt; Tib. *lama*)   a spiritual guide or teacher; one who shows a disciple the path to liberation and enlightenment; in *tantra,* one's teacher seen as inseparable from the meditational deity and the three jewels of refuge.

guru-yoga (Skt.)   the fundamental tantric practice whereby one's *guru* is seen as identical with the buddhas, one's personal meditational deity and the essential nature of one's own mind.

hatha-yoga (Skt.)   physical exercises designed to make the body more supple, thereby helping to remove blockages impeding the proper flow of the energy-winds; used in certain practices related to the *vajra* body.

Heruka Chakrasamvara (Tib. Kor-lo dem-chog)   male meditational deity of highest *yoga tantra.*

highest *yoga tantra* (Skt. *anuttara-yoga tantra*)   the fourth and supreme division of tantric practice, consisting of generation and completion stages, capable of leading the practitioner to full enlightenment within one lifetime.

ignorance (Skt. *avidya;* Tib. *ma-rig-pa*)   the mistaken belief in the independent, self-existence of things; the delusion which is the root of *samsara* and the source of all suffering, eradicated by the wisdom of emptiness.

illusory body (Skt. *mayakaya;* Tib. *gyu-lu*)   a subtle bodily form generated through the practice of the completion stage of highest *yoga tantra.*

initiation   see empowerment

inner fire (Tib. *tum-mo*)   energy residing at the navel *chakra*, aroused during the completion stage of highest *yoga tantra* and used to bring the energy-winds into the central channel; also referred to as inner heat, psychic heat.

insight meditation (Skt. *vipashyana*)   investigation   of   and familiarization with the actual way in which things exist; used to develop the wisdom of emptiness.

intermediate state   see *bardo*.

Kalachakra (Tib. Du-kor)   literally, cycle of time; male meditational deity of highest *yoga tantra* whose practice contains instructions in medicine, astronomy, etc. as well as the path to enlightenment.

karma (Skt.)   action; the working of cause and effect whereby positive actions produce happiness and negative actions produce suffering.

kaya (Skt.)   see three bodies of a *buddha*.

kundalini (Skt.)   blissful energy dormant within the physical body, aroused through tantric practice and used to generate penetrative insight into the true nature of reality.

lama (Tib.; Skt. *guru*)   a spiritual guide or teacher in the buddhist traditions of Tibet; cf. *guru*.

liberation   see *nirvana*.

Madhyamika (Skt.)   the middle way; a system of analysis founded by Nagarjuna, based on the *Perfection of Wisdom Sutras* of Shakyamuni Buddha, considered to be the supreme presentation of the wisdom of emptiness; cf. middle way.

mahamudra (Skt.)   the great seal; a profound system of meditation upon the mind and the ultimate nature of reality.

mahasiddha (Skt.)   a greatly accomplished tantric practitioner.

mandala (Skt.)   a circular diagram symbolic of the entire universe; the abode of a meditational deity, understood as the emanation of the wisdom of that deity; figuratively, one's personal surroundings seen as a reflection of one's state of mind.

Manjushri (Tib. Jam-pel-yang) male meditational deity embodying fully enlightened wisdom.

mantra (Skt.)   literally, protection of the mind; Sanskrit syllables recited in conjunction with the practice of a particular meditational deity and embodying the qualities of that deity.

Marpa (1012–1096)   founder of the Ka-gyu tradition of Tibetan

Buddhism; renowned tantric master and translator; disciple of Naropa and *guru* of Milarepa.

meditation   the process of becoming thoroughly familiar with beneficial states of mind through both analytic investigation and single-pointed concentration.

meditational deity (Tib. *yi-dam*)   a male or female figure embodying a particular aspect of the fully enlightened experience and used as the focus of concentration and identification in *tantra*.

middle way   the view presented in Shakyamuni Buddha's *Perfection of Wisdom Sutras* and elucidated by Nagarjuna that all phenomena are dependent arisings, thereby avoiding the mistaken extremes of self-existence and non-existence, or eternalism and nihilism; cf. *Madhyamika*.

Milarepa (1040–1123)   foremost disciple of Marpa, famous for his intense practice, devotion to his *guru*, attainment of enlightenment and his many songs of spiritual realization.

nadi (Skt.)   see channels.

Nagarjuna   Indian *mahasiddha* who elucidated the *Perfection of Wisdom Sutras* of Shakyamuni Buddha and founded the Madhyamika school of philosophy.

Nalanda   North Indian monastic university; one of the major sources of the tantric lineages that spread to Tibet.

Naropa   eleventh century Indian *mahasiddha* who transmitted many profound tantric lineages including those of Heruka Chakrasamvara and Vajrayogini; disciple of Tilo-pa and *guru* of Marpa.

nirmanakaya (Skt.)   see emanation body.

nirvana (Skt.)   the state of complete liberation from *samsara*; the goal of the practitioner seeking his or her own freedom from suffering; 'lower *nirvana*' is used to refer to this state of self-liberation while 'higher *nirvana*' refers to the supreme attainment of the full enlightenment of buddhahood.

non-dual wisdom   the understanding of the actual way in which things exist, free of all dualistic conceptions; often used as a synonym for the wisdom of emptiness.

Panchen Lama (1570–1662)   The First Panchen Lama, who was a *guru* of the Fifth Dalai Lama, was the author of many teachings on both *sutra* and *tantra* including *Offering to the Spiritual Master* and the *mahamudra* text, *Main Path of the Conquerors*.

Perfection of Wisdom Sutras (Skt. *Prajnaparamita-sutra*) those teachings of Shakyamuni Buddha in which the wisdom of emptiness and the path of the *bodhisattva* are set forth.

preliminary practices (Tib. *ngön-dro*) the meditations designed to remove hindrances and accumulate a store of meritorious energy so that a disciple will have success in the practice of *tantra*.

prana (Skt.) see energy-winds.

pure land a state of existence outside *samsara* in which all conditions are favourable for becoming fully enlightened.

rebirth the entrance of consciousness into a new state of existence after death and, in some cases, the intermediate state; the aim of tantric practice is to free this process from the control of the delusions.

renunciation see definite emergence.

residential mind the very subtle mind, residing within the heart *chakra*, the continuity of which passes from lifetime to lifetime together with its very subtle supporting energy-wind.

sadhana (Skt.) method of accomplishment; the step-by-step instructions for practising the meditations related to a particular meditational deity.

samadhi (Skt.) a state of deep meditative absorption; single-pointed concentration on the actual nature of things, free from discursive thought and dualistic conceptions.

sambhogakaya (Skt.) see enjoyment body.

samsara (Skt.) cyclic existence; the recurring cycle of death and rebirth under the control of ignorance and fraught with suffering.

sangha (Skt.) spiritual community; the third of the three jewels of refuge.

secret *mantra* the tantric teachings of Buddhism; cf. *tantrayana*.

seed-syllable in tantric visualizations, a Sanskrit syllable arising out of emptiness and out of which the meditational deity in turn arises.

self-cherishing the self-centred attitude of considering one's own happiness to be more important than everyone else's; the main obstacle to be overcome in the development of *bodhicitta*.

self-existence the mistaken conception that things exist independently from their own side rather than being dependent upon causes, conditions, parts and the process of conceptual imputation; the wisdom of emptiness is the understanding that all things lack, or are empty of, even an atom of such self-existence.

Shakyamuni Buddha (563–483BC) fourth of the one thousand founding buddhas of this present world age; born a prince of the Shakya Clan in North India, he taught the *sutra* and *tantra* path to liberation and full enlightenment; founder of what came to be known as Buddhism.

shunyata (Skt.)   see emptiness.

Six Yogas of Naropa   teachings dealing mainly with the completion stage practices of highest *yoga tantra*.

sutra (Skt.)   a discourse of Shakyamuni Buddha; the pre-tantric division of buddhist teachings stressing the cultivation of *bodhicitta* and the practices of the six perfections: generosity, discipline, patience, effort, meditative concentration and wisdom.

sutrayana (Skt.)   the pre-tantric vehicle of Buddhism, leading to the attainment of full enlightenment over three countless æons through the practice of the six perfections; hence, also called the perfection vehicle (Skt. *paramitayana*).

taking refuge   turning one's mind towards a valid source of protection from the sufferings of *samsara*; in Buddhism this involves entrusting oneself to the three jewels of *buddha*, *dharma* and *sangha*.

tantra (Skt.)   literally, thread or continuity; the texts of the secret *mantra* teachings of Buddhism; often used to refer to these teachings themselves.

tantrayana (Skt.)   the post-*sutra* vehicle of Buddhism, capable of leading to the attainment of full enlightenment within one lifetime; hence, also called the lightning vehicle; *vajrayana*; *mantrayana*.

tantric master   a *guru* qualified to grant empowerment and lead disciples along the tantric path to enlightenment.

Tara (Tib. Dolma)   female meditational deity embodying the virtuous conduct of enlightened beings; referred to as the mother of the buddhas of the past, present and future.

three bodies of a *buddha* (Skt. *tri-kaya*) an enlightened being's unobstructed mind *(dharmakaya)*, appearance to highly realized bodhisattvas *(sambhogakaya)* and appearance to ordinary beings *(nirmanakaya)*; cf. truth body, enjoyment body and emanation body.

three jewels of refuge   *buddha, dharma* and *sangha.*

three principal aspects of the path   the essential teachings of the *sutra* path to enlightenment; cf. definite emergence, *bodhicitta* and emptiness.

Tilopa   tenth century *mahasiddha* and *guru* of Naropa; source of many lineages of secret *mantra* teachings.

totality   the state in which all limitations to the full development and expression of one's inner potential have been removed; Lama Yeshe's non-traditional synonym for enlightenment or buddhahood.

truth body (Skt. *dharmakaya*)   the mind of a fully enlightened being, free of all coverings, remaining meditatively absorbed in the direct perception of emptiness while simultaneously cognizing all phenomena; cf. three bodies of a *buddha.*

tum-mo (Tib.)   see inner fire.

Tzongkhapa (1357–1417)   founder of the Ge-luk tradition of Tibetan Buddhism; revitalizer of many *sutra* and *tantra* lineages as well as the monastic tradition in Tibet.

vajra body   the system of channels, energy-winds and drops existing within a human being's ordinary physical body and activated through the practice of highest *yoga tantra*, thereby leading to the arousal of an extremely subtle and blissful state of mind (cf. clear light) capable of generating a penetrative wisdom that can eradicate delusions from the mind.

Vajradhara (Tib. Dorje-chang)   male meditational deity; the form through which Shakyamuni Buddha reveals the teachings of secret *mantra.*

Vajrasattva (Tib. Dorje-sempa)   male meditational deity; a major tantric purification practice for removing obstacles created by negative *karma* and the breaking of one's vows; cf. preliminary practices.

Vajrayogini (Tib. Dorje-naljorma)   female meditational deity, associated with Heruka Chakrasamvara.

vehicle (Skt. *yana*)   the means whereby a practitioner is led to his or her desired spiritual attainment; cf. *sutrayana* and *tantrayana.*

visualization   the use of creative imagination in meditation, as in the generation of oneself as a particular meditational deity;

despite the term used, visualization is not limited to vision, but involves the full creative sphere of one's imaging abilities.

wisdom (Skt. *prajna;* Tib. *she-rab)*   the unmistaken understanding of things; specifically, the insight into emptiness: the actual way in which things exist; the antidote to ignorance; symbolized by Manjushri.

yidam (Tib.)   see meditational deity.

yoga (Skt.)   the spiritual discipline to which one 'yokes' oneself in order to achieve full integration of body and mind.

yogi (Skt.)   a male practitioner of *yoga;* a tantric adept.

yogini (Skt.)   a female practitioner of *yoga:* a tantric adept.

Selected Additional Reading

Aryasura's Aspiration and a Meditation on Compassion, H. H. the Dalai Lama, Dharamsala: Library of Tibetan Works and Archives, 1979.

Bodhisattva of Compassion: The Mystical Tradition of Kuan Yin, J. Blofeld, Boston: Shambhala, 1978.

The Crystal and the Way of Light (Sutra, Tantra and Dzogchen), Namkhai Norbu, London: Arkana Books, 1986.

The Cult of Tara: Magic and Ritual in Tibet, Stephan Beyer, Berkeley: University of California Press, 1978.

Dakini Teachings: Padmasambhava's Oral Instructions to Lady Tsogyal, Padmasambhava, Boston: Shambhala, 1990.

The Dawn of Tantra, Chögyam Trungpa, Boston: Shambhala, 1975.

Death, Intermediate State and Rebirth in Tibetan Buddhism, Lati Rinbochay and J. Hopkins (trans.), Ithaca: Snow Lion, 1980.

Deity Yoga, H. H. the Dalai Lama, Tsong-ka-pa, and J. Hopkins (trans.), Ithaca: Snow Lion, 1981.

The Door of Liberation, Geshe Wangyal, Boston: Wisdom Publications, 1994.

The Door to Satisfaction, Lama Zopa Rinpoche, Boston: Wisdom Publications, 1994.

Drinking the Mountain Stream, Lama Kunga Rinpoche and Brian Cutillo, Boston: Wisdom Publications, 1995.

The Essential Nectar: Meditations on the Buddhist Path, Geshe Rabten, trans. M. Willson, Boston: Wisdom Publications, 1984.

The Flight of the Garuda: Teachings of the Dzokchen Tradition of Tibetan Buddhism, Keith Dowman (trans.), Boston: Wisdom Publications, 1994.

Foundations of Tibetan Mysticism (According to the Esoteric Teachings of the Great Mantra OM MANI PADME HUM*)*, Lama Govinda, London: Rider, 1969.

A Guide to the Bodhisattva's Way of Life, Shantideva, S. Batchelor (trans.), Dharamsala: Library of Tibetan Works and Archives, 1979.

Highest Yoga Tantra, Daniel Cozort, Ithaca: Snow Lion, 1986.

How to Meditate: A Practice Guide, Kathleen McDonald, Boston: Wisdom Publications, 1984.

The Hundred Thousand Songs of Milarepa, Garma C. C. Chang (trans.), Boston: Shambhala, 1977.

In Praise of Tara: Songs to the Saviouress, Martin Willson (trans.), Boston: Wisdom Publications, 1986.

The Jewel in the Lotus: A Guide to the Buddhist Traditions of Tibet, Stephen Batchelor, Boston: Wisdom Publications, 1987.

Journey Without Goal: The Tantric Wisdom of Buddha, Chögyam Trungpa, Boulder: Prajna, 1981.

Kalachakra Tantra, Geshe Ngawang Dhargyey, Dharamsala: Library of Tibetan Works and Archives, 1985.

The Kalachakra Tantra: Rite of Initiation, H. H. the Dalai Lama and J. Hopkins, Boston: Wisdom Publications, 1985.

Kindness, Clarity and Insight, H. H. the Dalai Lama, J. Hopkins (trans.), Ithaca: Snow Lion, 1984.

Liberation in the Palm of Your Hand, Pabongka Rinpoche, Boston: Wisdom Publications, 1991.

The Life and Liberation of Padmasambhava by Yeshe Tsogyal, (trans.) K. Douglas and G. Bays, Berkeley: Dharma Publishing, 1979.

The Life and Teaching of Naropa, H. V. Guenther, Boston: Shambhala, 1986.

Life and Teachings of Lama Tsong Khapa, Robert Thurman (ed.), Dharamsala: Library of Tibetan Works and Archives, 1982.

The Life of Milarepa, L. P. Lhalungpa (trans.), New York: Arkana Books, 1979.

The Lion's Roar: An Introduction to Tantra, Chögyam Trungpa, Boston: Shambhala, 1992.

Magic Dance: The Display of the Self-Nature of the Five Wisdom Dakinis, Trinley Norbu, New York: Jewel Publishing, 1985.

Mahayana Purification, Brian Beresford (trans.), Dharamsala: Library of Tibetan Works and Archives, 1980.

Mandala, J. and M. Argüelles, Boston: Shambhala, 1972.

Mantras: Sacred Words of Power, J. Blofeld, London: Mandala, 1977.

The Preliminary Practices, Geshe Rabten, Dharamsala: Library of Tibetan Works and Archives, 1974.

Preparing for Tantra, Tsongkapa, Howell, New Jersey: Mahayana Sutra and Tantra Press, 1995.

The Secret Oral Teachings on Generating the Deity, Ven. Gyarrul Rinpoche, Taipei: SMC Publishing, 1992.

Selected Works of the Dalai Lamas, Glenn Mullin (trans.), Ithaca: Snow Lion, various years.

Six Yogas of Naropa and Teachings on Mahamudra, Garma C. C. Chang, Ithaca: Snow Lion, 1963.

Sky Dancer: The Secret Life and Songs of the Lady Yeshe Tsogyel, K. Dowman, London: Arkana Books, 1984.

Tantra in Tibet: The Great Exposition of Secret Mantra (Volume I) by Tsong-ka-pa, H. H. the Dalai Lama and J. Hopkins (trans.), London: Unwin Hyman, 1977.

The Tantric Distinction, J. Hopkins, Boston: Wisdom Publications, 1984.

The Tantric Mysticism of Tibet, J. Blofeld, New York: Arkana Books, 1970.

The Tantric Path of Purification: Vajrasattva Practice and Retreat Manual, Lama Yeshe, Boston: Wisdom Publications, 1994.

Tantric Practice in Nying-ma, Khetsun Sangpo Rinbochay, Ithaca: Snow Lion, 1986.

Tibetan Buddhism From the Ground Up, B. Alan Wallace, Boston: Wisdom Publications, 1993.

The Torch of Certainty, Jamgön Kongtrül, Boston: Shambhala, 1977.

Transforming Problems Into Happiness, Lama Zopa Rinpoche, Boston: Wisdom Publications, 1992.

The Wheel of Time: The Kalachakra in Context, Geshe Sopa et al., Ithaca: Snow Lion, 1985.

Wisdom Energy, Lama Yeshe and Lama Zopa Rinpoche, Boston: Wisdom Publications, 1982.

Wisdom Energy 2, Lama Yeshe et al., Boston: Wisdom Publications, 1979.

Women of Wisdom, Tsultrim Allione, London: Arkana Books, 1984.

Wisdom Publications

Wisdom Publications, a not-for-profit publisher, is dedicated to making available authentic Buddhist works for the benefit of all. We publish translations of the sutras and tantras, commentaries and teachings of past and contemporary Buddhist masters, and original works by the world's leading Buddhist scholars. We publish our titles with the appreciation of Buddhism as a living philosophy and with the special commitment to preserve and transmit important works from all the major Buddhist traditions.

If you would like more information or a copy of our mail-order catalogue, please contact us at:

Wisdom Publications
199 Elm Street
Somerville, Massachusetts 02144-3195 USA
Telephone: (617) 776-7416
Fax: (617) 776-7841
E-mail: info@wisdompubs.org
Web Site: http://www.wisdompubs.org

THE WISDOM TRUST

As a not-for-profit publisher, Wisdom Publications is dedicated to the publication of fine Dharma books for the benefit of all sentient beings and dependent upon the kindness and generosity of sponsors in order to do so. If you would like to make a donation to Wisdom, please contact our Somerville office.

Thank you.

Wisdom Publications is a non-profit, charitable 501(c)(3) organization and a part of the Foundation for the Preservation of the Mahayana Tradition (FPMT).

The Foundation for the Preservation of the Mahayana Tradition

The Foundation for the Preservation of the Mahayana Tradition (FPMT) is an international network of Buddhist centers and activities dedicated to the transmission of Mahayana Buddhism as a practiced and living tradition. The FPMT was founded in 1975 by Lama Thubten Yeshe and Lama Thubten Zopa Rinpoche. It is composed of monasteries, retreat centers, communities, publishing houses and healing centers, all functioning as a means to benefit others. Teachings, such as those presented in *Introduction to Tantra*, are given at many of the centers.

To receive a complete listing of these centers as well as news about the activities throughout this global network, please write requesting a complimentary copy of the MANDALA newsmagazine:

FPMT INTERNATIONAL OFFICE
P.O. Box 1778
Soquel, California 95073
Telephone: (408) 476-8435
Fax: (408) 476-4823

Care of Dharma Books

Dharma books contain the teachings of the Buddha; they have the power to protect against lower rebirth and to point the way to liberation. Therefore, they should be treated with respect—kept off the floor and places where people sit or walk—and not stepped over. They should be covered or protected for transporting and kept in a high, clean place separate from more "mundane" materials. Other objects should not be placed on top of Dharma books and materials. Licking the fingers to turn pages is considered bad form (and negative karma). If it is necessary to dispose of Dharma materials, they should be burned rather than thrown in the trash. When burning Dharma texts, it is considered skillful to first recite a prayer or mantra, such as OM, AH, HUNG. Then, you can visualize the letters of the texts (to be burned) absorbing into the AH, and the AH absorbing into you. After that, you can burn the texts.

These considerations may also be kept in mind for Dharma artwork, as well as the written teachings and artwork of other religions.

The Tantric Path of Purification
The Yoga Method of Heruka Vajrasattva
Lama Yeshe

"We have to understand that the qualities of Vajrasattva are already within us. But our realizations, method and wisdom are limited. These have to be developed by our identifying with the limitless pure energy of the archetype. Instead of thinking of ourselves as limited, hopeless sentient beings, we have to recognize our incredible potential. We can free ourselves from the confusion of uncontrolled concepts. We can develop our consciousness to the limitless states of universal compassion, universal love, universal wisdom, universal freedom. The Vajrasattva practice can lead us beyond ego, beyond grasping, and beyond the dualistic mind."—Lama Yeshe

In this wonderful book, Lama Thubten Yeshe explains one of the most powerful mental purification practices in the vast array of Buddhist meditations. Included is an entire section of complete retreat instructions—required reading for anybody who undertakes a retreat in the Tibetan tradition.

$15.00, 344 pages, 0-86171-020-7

Reincarnation
The Boy Lama
Vicki Mackenzie

The Boy Lama is the reincarnation of Lama Thubten Yeshe, one of the most significant Tibetan lamas in the transmission of Tibetan Buddhism to the Western world.

Born in Tibet in 1935, Lama Yeshe became a monk at the age of six. In 1959, he was forced from his homeland into exile in India by the Chinese invasion and began teaching Westerners in 1967. He founded the world-wide Foundation for the Preservation of the Mahayana Tradition (FPMT), which now has more than 80 centers and thousands of students in 18 countries.

Lama Yeshe passed away in 1984. He was reincarnated in Spain in 1985 as Lama Tenzin Osel Rinpoche and was confirmed by the Dalai Lama the following year. This book tells the remarkable story of Lama Yeshe's life, death, and rebirth, while explaining the controversial phenomenon of reincarnation in a clear, engaging, and practical way.

"*Reincarnation: The Boy Lama* was the first account I read of a Tibetan Lama reincarnating as a western boy. A dazzling and inspiring adventure story."
—Bernardo Bertolucci, film director, *The Little Buddha*

$16.95, 228 pages, 0-86171-108-4